What Readers are Saying!

"Exciting, makes the spirit soar!"

"I like your fresh style and approach. You handle channeling and your angelic encounters very carefully and sensitively; it's suspenseful reading."

"Dramatically written. Hard to put down."

"This book has the quality to reach a wide audience because of its content and the author's ability to bring the message to the reader."

"A must read for all Truth students."

"I wish you many inspiring angelic contacts and look forward to reading more."

"Lots of luck with your new best seller."

My Secret Life with
an Angel

Earth in the Seventh Circle

My Secret Life
with
an Angel

Earth in the Seventh Circle

Julia M. Busch

 *Kosmic Kurrents*

is an imprint of ANTI-AGING PRESS, INC.

P.O. BOX 141489 • CORAL GABLES, FLORIDA 33114 • USA

The purpose of this book is to offer knowledge as given to the author by the Cosmic Angelic Forces. Any application of the concepts and/or information contained in this book is done solely at the discretion of the reader. This is a true story. Names of persons have been changed to protect the right of privacy.

Kosmic Kurrents books are available at special discounts for bulk purchases for premiums, fund-raising, sales promotions or educational use. Special editions or book excerpts can be composed to specification. For details, contact:

Kosmic Kurrents
P.O. Box 141489
Coral Gables, Florida 33114 USA
(305)662-3928   Fax (305)661-4123
email: julia@icanect.net

Foreign rights interests please contact Dieter Hagenbach, GAIA Media Ag, Spalenvorstadt 13, CH 4003, Basel, Switzerland. email: gaiamediaag@access.ch.

Publisher's Cataloging in Publication

Busch, Julia M.
    My Secret Life with an Angel : earth in the seventh circle /
Julia M. Busch.
    p. cm.
    Includes index.
    Preassigned LCCN: 96-79343.
    ISBN: 1-886369-16-X.

    1. Angels. 2. Spirit Writing. 3. Channeling (Spiritualism). 4.
Soul. 5. Karma. I. Title.

BF1301.B87 1997   133.9'3
                                        QBI96-40779

Dedicated in Love to the Earth
and to you of the Earth who
by your presence
have made the long-term commitment
to learning that all Truth and Light
lies in Love and Compassion,
and all Love and Compassion
lies in Truth and Light.
Hammal Cahone,
Head of the Cosmic Angelic Force.

Acknowledgments

Thank you...

Della Attisani for scrupulous editing.

Scherley Busch Photography for still another great cover photo.

Hollye Davidson for more than I can ever express.

Wally Engelhard and Shirlee Dreyer of Engelhard Printing and Joan Mangrum of Braun-Brumfield, Inc. for meticulous production.

It was a pleasure.

Table of Contents

About the Author

Described as a Renaissance woman, Julia Busch is the multifaceted, multitalented publisher of Anti-Aging Press and Kosmic Kurrents, editor of two newsletters, *The H-Files: Conferences with a Cosmic Angel,* containing channeled information, and *So Young,* dedicated to a youthful body, mind and spirit.

She has authored ten titles, including holistic health and healing titles: <u>Powerful Prayer Secrets</u> and <u>Power Color,</u> (coauthored with Hollye Davidson), <u>Positively Young</u>, <u>Facelift Naturally</u>, and <u>Youth and Skin Secrets Revealed</u>. Her beauty classic <u>Treat Your Face Like a Salad</u> (alternately titled <u>The Home Guide to Natural Beauty Care</u>, Berkley Books: New York) was a featured alternate selection of the Doubleday Health Book Club.

Ms. Busch is a jewelry designer, registered for more than 20 years under the trademark of *Julia,* a painter, draftsman, poet and columnist. She studied voice and opera at Juilliard School of Music, received a degree in art history from the University of Miami, FL, where she taught drawing and composition while lecturing in humanities at Dade Community College. She has taught painting, sculpture, drawing and jewelry-making, and exhibited in these media.

Postgraduate work in art history was undertaken at the University of Miami and at Columbia University NY.

Ms. Busch has been listed in <u>Who's Who in American Art</u>, <u>Who's Who of American Women</u>, <u>Who's Who of Women of the World</u> and <u>Personalities of the South</u>. Her first book, a critical analysis and survey of the art and art technology of the 1960s, <u>A Decade of Sculpture</u> (Philadelphia Art Alliance) is a reference standard.

Ms. Busch researches beauty in its all its aspects, encompassing a lifelong interest in health and well-being on all levels. She has written on a variety of topics, including the dilemma of aging in a youth-oriented society.

She was art critic for *Ideas* magazine, has written for the *Art Journal,* and contributed on health matters to *InnerSelf* and *Let's Live,* among others. At present she writes *Beating the Clock,* a column on the internet publication *Wednesday on the Web.*

Ms. Busch holds a certificate in aromatherapy, has cohosted *Youthfully Yours* on Talk America, and is an expert in the area of holistic health, anti-aging, and youth extension. Her titles have been translated into German, Finnish, Danish, Czechoslovakian, Thai, Chinese, Bulgarian and for the East Indian English-language market.

I
Cosmic Angels on Earth

Chapter 1

An Angel Appears

My introduction to an angel came as most answers to prayers do—as a surprise after a long search.

The night was warm and expansive with the soft, sultry expectant undertones that only a Miami night can embrace. Wrapped in a sense of safety, I was comfortably unwinding after a productive day of painting, sketching and teaching when an audible voice directed a message to me—not *through* me but *to* me...

"Dearest Julia, I am Hammal Cahone, Head of the Cosmic Angelic Force. My name is not of a language but of universal sounds, translating to Nameless One." The presentation was undeniably masculine.

"I belong to a new consciousness that is coming to humanity—a consciousness that has waited for the right time to present itself. I am here to relay a new dimension that will expand the boundaries of humankind, expounding new light coming into this solar system's reign of thought."

Stunned, I thought of Noah, Moses and all the characters in the Old Testament who were on a first name basis with angelic beings. How did I rate?

Almost dumbfounded, but blessed with an unstoppable tongue, I tried to order my mental fragments into sentences. What new consciousness and dimension? Expand the solar system's mental boundaries? What a fascinating concept—certainly everyone, every realm has boundaries.

I thought of *Star Trek* and mentally launched a probe into outer space only to be told in no uncertain terms that the new spacial expansion did not belong to the physical world. Hammal was not an extraterrestrial. He was of the spirit, a cosmic angel—from a very different realm. Hammal was in fact the head of a particular angelic force.

Hammal laughed, graciously acknowledging my surprise at his sudden appearance, and confided that we were supposed to meet several years in the future but, as usual, I had forced a premature meeting. More questions flooded in. Had we known each other before? I later found out we had.

Without a pause, he continued. "Recently there has been an upsurge by part of the world in recognition of angels; next will come an upsurge against. But it is important that those who could be made aware of angels are made aware."

My warm, safe feeling was slipping away. I felt the urge to do something, to somehow protect the angels and their knowledge. But high school physics flashed: there is no action without an equal and opposite reaction. I quietly listened and quickly slid my pen and note-pad from the table next to my bed. As the revelations unfolded, I wrote...

"Throughout time, we have touched upon the earth." Hammal continued. "Many already know of our existence and how to call us, but if our total function was known and understood, then much more could be accomplished.

"Much vaster than one would ever suspect, the angelic forces are controlled by an intensity far greater than ever would be imagined. There are at least 20,000 separate forces that we could touch upon, and countless more."

I felt the impact of his words but couldn't begin to comprehend the scope or power of his realm. Little did I realize that what Hammal had to say this night would be expanded in ways I could never fathom.

"All angels," he continued, "are good and do good works, but angels do not *usually* make good things happen. Good is *supposed* to happen. It is, however, through the protection of the angelic force that the good that is supposed to happen, *does* happen."

My security was beginning to return. I wrote as quickly as I could using abbreviations and symbols, intent on catching every syllable and inflection. I quietly thanked goodness, or whatever, for making me pick up a speed writing book way back when.

Hammal's strong, steady sounds continued to unfold the message. "At this time, the earth is returning to the knowledge it has lost for seven circles and is again advancing to the seventh circle to gain new knowledge," he said.

Dante's *Inferno* darted through my thoughts.

"The seventh circle usually means annihilation," Hammal explained. "The last seven earths have been destroyed, but we do not have to destruct when we change circles. There are levels of learning to avoid this devastation."

So much for security. Cold fear crawled up my ankles determined to meet the air that was filling my brain. What if we don't learn what we need to learn? I said nothing, steadied myself and kept writing.

"The reason the earth is now again on the way to destruction is because the need for knowledge, the need for truth, is disappearing just as a person who doesn't want to live has no need for life."

This made sense—if you don't need life, you don't need an earth. But I wasn't comfortable with the turn this message was taking. I started on a new page.

"We of the Cosmic Angelic Force are trying to repair humankind's thoughts and allow humanity to be free to go to the first circle on the next level *intact*," his voice was deliberate and hopeful.

As I struggled to understand, *The Twilight Zone* joined *Star Trek* and Dante's *Inferno*. More thoughts and pictures flooded into my head, including out-of-the-body etheric surgeries being performed on an ailing earth and humanity—bizarre imaginings recollected from an offbeat documentary.

"At present," Hammal continued in a sobering tone that noted my discomfort, "we are attempting to go back to Atlantis for the knowledge we need.

"In finding out about humankind as a *whole*, humanity can open its mind to channel more freely and be more tolerant of things unseen."

So Atlantis was real. I was elated. I had always believed in the myth, but now its physical reality was acknowledged. And the knowledge Atlantis possessed was needed for our future. The notion was comforting.

I had always pictured white robes, crystals, light, and radiant color when I imagined Atlantis, recoiling from conversations that implicated the civilization in negativity.

"Atlantis was one of many seeds planted here to evolve into higher knowledge," Hammal revealed. "The civilization was never intended to last for very long."

Later, Hammal disclosed that Atlantis had perished because it was too positive to exist on the earth.

I prayed the earth could now accept the knowledge it needed.

Uneasy with the alternative, I took comfort in knowing there was a plan.

Hammal's introductory message had been told in simple sentences. In retrospect, I realized they were doors to future volumes of information.

"I'm following him nicely," I thought—that is, right up until he said..."Humankind has misunderstood the meaning of the circles. Nothing on earth ever gets to eight. God is earth—god is debt. Debt is dead at eight. Infinity is nine."

"Wait a minute. You're losing me!" I mutely called unable to write, think and speak all at once.

"Eight is freedom from debt, or peace on earth," Hammal sped on. "Eight is the highest hope—when you have learned and you know. That is why eight is heaven on earth, when god, that is, debt, is eliminated."

"Wait...wait..."I was writing now as fast as I could.

"Once you get to eight, souls will be so finely attuned that earth, as it now exists, will not be needed. It will transform and another will take its place."

I was totally lost and Hammal was finished.

Thus, Hammal delivered the bombshell—a preamble to twenty plus years of cosmic revelations. Reflecting on these concepts has become part of my daily life and will continue for the rest of my life.

Hammal would eventually explain the circles and the numbers, but there was much to learn before I got there.

Chapter 2

One Angel Becomes Seven

A seer saw seven purple flames dancing like a crown over my head.

The seven flames were angels, Hammal and six more.

I clearly remember the night Hammal introduced the others. The events are as vivid as if it was all happening right now. I was standing in the kitchen, casually noting how the white walls and brown cabinets took on the mellow yellow cast of the light bulb when I began to see subtle changes in the light. It happened gradually, at first. Then suddenly the room was transformed to brilliant white. Hammal extended a greeting to announce his arrival. And we began to talk about several personal matters that I wished to resolve.

Minutes into the conversation, Unga (Oon-ga'), a close liaison to Hammal, made his presence known. This was my first awareness of another angel. I was told that he was guarded on either side by two very large, lean, black, thin-nosed dogs called Acaba (A-ka'-ba) and Avenu (A-vay'-nu). He was introduced as the Angel of Individual Guidance.

Hammal spoke, "Unga wants you to know his presence is around you and his dogs are now at your side. Acaba stands at your right, and Avenu shields your left. They will allow you to go to new levels and delve deeper with safety and guidance than you ever have before. Wherever you step, you will have instant protection. They will not lead you astray at any moment."

Unaware of the significance of Unga's gift, but flattered and surprised by his generous gesture, I warmly welcomed my new protectors. In retrospect, I can see that this was the first slender crack as the vault, slowly and carefully, rolled open to reveal the vast angelic army once heralded by Joan of Arc—along with a task that Hercules would have fled. With the presence of Acaba and Avenu, I felt substantial in a way I never did before.

"Unga wants you to know that you can call on him anytime for guidance regarding any individual and the direction the individual should take to help him or herself."

Not once did Unga speak aloud. As Head of the Cosmic Angelic Force, Hammal translated all information that came from and through other angels. This, he explained, was for the earth's protection. Hammal planned and interpreted what was needed and what could be accepted within the framework of humanity.

"It is I who marshal the Cosmic Angelic Force, a special angelic force on your behalf," he confided one day.

On my behalf...me, *personally?* Or was this another way of saying on behalf of the earth? I had questions. Boy, did I have questions. And each time I asked a question I had more questions. Seeds were being dropped. But like countless crumbs from a good loaf of Dijon rye, it would take many meetings before I got a taste of the loaf.

Unannounced to me, this was to be a night of ceremony. My formal introduction to Hammal's highest liaisons had been scheduled. His cabinet was being assembled with the ritual of a presidential inauguration. I was tutored in etiquette that required me to address each angel by name and title; after which I was to ask, "Help me to know of your function."

I had already been introduced to Hammal Cahone (Hammal' Ka-hone'), The Untitled One, and Unga, Angel of Individual Guidance. Now it was time to meet Mantra (Man-tra'), Speaker of the Soul.

The ceremony was awkward for me. Its impromptu nature afforded me no chance to practice my part. I continually stumbled over the script, my hastily scrawled names and the titles of the participants. And my head was reeling in the power that surrounded me.

As tutored, I asked, "Mantra, Speaker of the Soul, tell me of your function."

And Hammal translated. The words were stilted and formal, but the tone was gentle and reassuring, "I am Mantra, Speaker of the Soul. I am of eternal sound. I am to be asked for help in unification and balance. Any need that arises in this area may be worked through me."

I was in familiar territory. I knew the value of a mantra. Curious...that this angel's name was the same.

And I was no stranger to the unifying, balancing vibration of sound—or its power. Years at Juilliard School of Music and private study with my beloved voice teacher Marta Modern had refined my ear and tonal placement, and sent me running from New York's City Center when the soprano lead in "Girl of the Golden West" was a quarter of a tone flat. Yes, I understood the power of sound.

Mantra continued, "Although if you, for some reason, need my help in any other area, or need my viewpoint, I would most appreciatively assist you." He went on to say, "I work from within outward—from the soul to manifestation.

"As different currents and problems with other universes or individuals arise, I will go wherever I am needed to create new forms and transmute the things that need to be transmuted."

Mantra was moving beyond my mental boundaries. The territory felt familiar, but I couldn't put a hook into anything tangible. I believed in magic. The world was filled with inexplicable change. Just start with the basics—seeds magically transmute to plants. All of life itself is magic—this was my hook. Intuition told me there was much more to his meaning, but I had a hook.

Mantra kept speaking, "You may ask me to work on an individual problem and leave me to my work. It will be eternal work, and you may ask me to stop when you feel the time for its closing."

Eternal work? *I* am to be able to ask *him* to stop?

I listened, intent on comprehension. Every sentence held volumes. Later I would return to my notes to discover meanings, levels of understanding and nuances opening in endless kaleidoscopic bursts, like fireworks on the Fourth of July. I pondered for days, weeks, months. With each new piece of knowledge, with each new crumb of information, more dimensions were revealed.

Icail (I-kale'), Bringer of Foreseen Light, was next to speak. He presented himself. Once again, I read, "Icail, Bringer of Foreseen Light, tell me of your function."

Once again, Hammal translated—the ceremony was moving at a stately pace—"I, Icail, bring you the knowledge to help you with what is to come. I bring you also its opposite, the knowledge that has gone...which for me becomes foreseen light."

As he spoke, the room dissolved. I moved from a time-space-place into what seemed to be endless dimension where I could touch everything and nothing. I *was* all time, all space... Dicken's *Christmas Carol* whizzed through my brain. I was reeling under the power of these majestic entities who had no physical form, only immense presence. *I* felt transmuted and thought I had an idea why Acaba and Avenu were with me. But I hadn't a clue. I, at this time, could never have comprehended their value and there was no time to ponder. Samon (Sa-mone'), Translator to the Physical, was being introduced.

Formalities were exchanged. And through Hammal, Samon spoke. "I, Samon, translate the basic realities to humanity from a higher world. I simplify the reality of Cosmic Truth. I am going to help you to understand the spherical force and movement so that someday it can be broken down for earthly knowledge. We'll be doing a book together."

Samon is here working with me now, as are all the others.

Then Jake (Ja-kay'), Speaker of the Lost and Director of the Will, spoke out. And a speaker he was. Forcefully, he unveiled his angelic function with a power unlike the others. "I am the healer of pain, which is the lack of directed will. It is I, Julia, who have been reminding you of the work that is to be done."

I gasped. This put my recent waking and sleeping visions of suffocating tidal waves into an uncomfortable perspective.

Jake went on, "If you have any questions of what is to be done relative to deprived, lost, unbalanced or individual souls, or if you need to find new answers concerning the lost souls...I mean to help you in understanding all aspects, and to guide you toward the everlasting conscience of the universe."

His message struck another frightening note. I didn't know why.

"I will protect all that you cannot, or do not have the time for. I function throughout the universe with the angelic force. I may help those with diseases caused by the nonacceptance of one's own soul. But I am *never* one you tell to stop." With that he ended.

Even for a ravenous information seeker like myself, this last message with all its intensity and innuendo threw me into mental and emotional overload. I needed breathe, to rebalance, but the introductions were not yet complete.

I read my script for the final time, "Farrse (Farr-say'), Bringer of Universal Colors, tell me of your function."

He answered, "I, Farrse, work mainly with light throughout the total cosmic universe or whatever you choose to call it.

I bring to you not only color and vision; I shed new light on thought."

With that, the introductions were over. I had been introduced to Hammal's firsts in command, his advisors, his lieutenants. I learned that we had all worked together before and continue to work on many levels, past, present, and future, simultaneously in many universes. I learned that Farrse and I had know each other in China where we had incarnated at the same time. I was told that all the angels came from different cosmos, plus some more odd bits of information.

To my surprise, Hammal also revealed that the knowledge, being relayed to him through the vast spherical angelic forces, would become *reality* once it was brought to the earth. For this reason, Hammal carefully interpreted all incoming data.

So everything I experienced here tonight was resounding throughout the earth. Those who could recognize the truth would.

Soon I would also learn that each angel protected a different continent or section of the earth, but for a reason I would never have suspected.

Hammal was carefully laying out my awakening, carefully meting out the information I could handle. He was building the skeleton over which he would drape the sinew and flesh of the situation that he and the Cosmic Angelic Force were here to address. But all in good angelic time.

In closing, Hammal advised, "When you need assistance, call each angel by name and then by title to be sure the proper vibration is set in motion."

The evening's plan had been fulfilled and, for the time being, the room returned to mellow yellow.

Chapter 3

A Cryptic Message

"Dearest Julia, I am here to set straight a plan that has been lost or mistaken for centuries."

Hammal Cahone

The early meetings were filled with the pomp and passion one would expect from a powerful personage, the commander of a mighty multitude. Each conference was orchestrated to strike a different chord, programmed to apply more pressure, to awaken a new set of feelings and an ever-growing sense of crisis. Even so, I continued to manage a semblance of self and maintain a tenuous balance.

But tonight would change all that. This night's meeting began unlike any Hammal had commanded to date.

Almost immediately, I was forcibly swept up to a dizzying pinnacle where the air was electric and dark cumulous clouds rumbled their turmoil. The smell of ozone seared my nostrils and the soft hairs on my arms tugged at my skin.

Hammal's tone was urgent. He repeated, "Dearest Julia, I am here to set straight a plan that has been lost or mistaken for centuries...I refer to the volume of adversaries, the unbalanced components which build negativity and block the incoming light."

I quickly noted that light means knowledge.

"I am talking about the mass, and growing mass, of alienated and confused souls—lost souls who fly by day and night, who torture others and who torture themselves—children of darkness who grieve and will continue to grieve through careless knowledge," Hammal was weighing his words carefully. Something critical was unfolding.

Light-headed and reeling in the intense rarefied air, I assumed that hordes of tormented souls had decided to band together to halt the incoming cosmic knowledge that Hammal and the Angelic Force were here to deliver.

Hammal's message was consuming. I strained to catch every word. But my day had been long and I was tired. Concerned that I lacked the intense concentration needed for this important communique, I ached to get into the problem and assess the situation quickly.

Who are these souls, what are their grievances, and why are they barricading incoming knowledge? I wanted to know, but I knew not to ask. I had learned that any interruption mid-message would break the incoming vibration and fragment the delivery. Hammal was explaining the problem from a cosmic overview. I bore down and tried harder to concentrate. I wasn't at the top of my form, and Hammal knew it. But the urgency of the situation demanded that he proceed.

"Before we can continue to achieve a higher goal or stature, we must first, through understanding and much compassion, balance the souls that grieve," he pressed on. "Until this is done, they will continue to build negativity and block the light.

"At this time, both darkness and light exist in your universe on an equal basis. Disasters, both natural and unnatural, have accelerated.

"Huge vortices, powerful cones of negative gravity are sucking alien powers—gasses and viruses—onto the earth. This is why strange sicknesses are increasing here. The aggregates of the huge masses who grieve form the huge vortices. They are functioning in the manner of the pyramids to draw in forces unnatural to the earth. The gasses and viruses of which I speak would not be problems elsewhere in the cosmos."

I could feel the power of these tormented, seething, inverted tornados—disembodied souls that were not voluntarily barricading the light, but helplessly lost in a situation that had gotten out of hand.

I thought of Hammal's earlier explanation, "The reason the earth is now, again, on the way to destruction is because the need for knowledge, the need for truth, is disappearing just as the person who doesn't want to live has no need for life."

"Is this what happens to souls who have let go of life and truth?" I wondered.

"Trouble is breaking out everywhere," Hammal went on. "The entire solar system, and beyond, is being thrown off course by the earth. And the earth itself is in a state where it can self-destruct," he paused to let the vibrations of his missive settle.

Rumblings in the earth had already begun. Violent storms, floods, mud slides, earthquakes, occurring worldwide, monthly and weekly, were newsworthy events. A hurricane would come to ravage my own home.

I still feel the fear as I recount those torturous weeks—my senses numb. Talk of tidal waves and storm surges surfaced while nature's impending violence poised over Miami, bringing visions of Jake, Speaker of the Lost. When the hurricane hit, each shutter and tree that slammed against the house reverberated Hammal's words, "disasters...natural and unnatural."

And throughout that turbulent night I strained, terrified, pressing my foot against the hallway door to counter the unanticipated gusts of wind that threatened our narrow, safe place in the interior of the house. The attic fan louvers fluttered nervously overhead, delivering strange smells from the attic.

Nikki, my high-strung, eighty-pound black standard poodle, eyes glazed, was ready to bolt, and Tofi, one of my black cats, panicked and ran to a less protected place to moan his horror along with the heaving trees. Thank god my trembling Yorkie Hairy was snuggled fast asleep in one of the pet carriers I had stacked and furnished with pillows.

"My kitty condos," I joked to my dearest friend Havah, who had left her own home and husband to cower with me on a six-foot foam rubber sofa seat and yoga mat throughout the dark, hot, paralyzing night.

Hammal's reassurance, earlier in the day, offered little comfort that we would make it through the impending hurricane. Still, we giggled like two kids with flashlights at a sleepover party, pretending not to be afraid as the wind shrieked it's unnerving, ever-accelerating high-pitched whine.

We gasped with each crack, crash or thud that threatened us from the world outside. And Hammal's message, "the earth itself is in a state where it can self-destruct," echoed throughout the fury.

I pictured tidal waves inundating Havah, me and all my beloved pets. And as I held my breath in terror, I could almost feel the choking water crush my lungs.

When the morning news announced our freedom to assess the damage, I tried to get my bearings in the strange, still, first-light that painted over the eerie, hollow forms of devastation.

A poinciana tree with a trunk two grown men could have embraced without touching hands was laying in huge sections in the torn driveway inches from the house. My thirty-foot Australian pines lay across the street they had lovingly sheltered. Ripped from the earth, they destroyed the drain field and held my six-foot fence high in their roots. I cautiously crept out onto the patio, ankle-deep in drenched debris. The roof had blown away and the screens were shredded.

Havah and I crawled from the front door over the tangled mess to the street. In payment for her kind companionship, a cypress had fallen onto her Lincoln Town Car.

As the days and weeks went on, garbage piled up in the streets. Diverted trucks and cars cut deep, muddy ruts into a neighbor's well-manicured lawn, avoiding my fallen pines in the center of the heavily trafficked road.

Less fortunate survivors, well-armed with guns, guarded their gaping, roofless homes and unprotected belongings from marauders. Canned foods were collected for those without, and bottled water was doled out. Day-to-day orderly life was in chaos. People were zombies. It would be years before the rapid, subtropical growth could cover the raped and wounded land-scape.

"Is this the way humanity has chosen to learn the value of life?" I questioned.

Thinking back to Hammal's cryptic warning, I heard him say, "It is time to establish purity of thought. A new change is coming and, with the absence of the millions and millions of grieving souls, much of the planned work can and *must* be accomplished."

Centuries of fire and brimstone had sent fearful indict-ments to humanity, but this was not Hammal's message. There was no accusation. "There is no hell," he confided to me one day. "Hell is only a confusion in the mind of the human race." Hammal was here to help the masses of lost souls, get the original plan for the earth on track, and help the human race to save itself.

There was much work needed. According to cosmic history, the earth had destructed seven times and was threaten-ing to do so again. Yet this time was different. This time the Cosmic Angelic Force had been sent. Hammal's instructions were clear.

The task was formidable and somehow I was a part of it.

31

Was I simply Hammal's scribe? Was my role to publish the information he brought out into the open or was there more? In the months to come, I learned that it didn't matter if the words were ever published. In just his telling, the vibration was set.

But I had to know more about the souls that gathered to block the light. Had they gotten there through "careless knowledge"? Why did darkness and light exist equally within our universe at this time? The unsolved riddle of the numbers and circles churned in my brain. More surprises, more questions were on their way.

Chapter 4

What Are Angels?

"Dearest Julia, An angel is a spirit of the soul—a messenger from the soul, or into the soul, from the heavens." Hammal Cahone

Hammal's manner was easy and unpressured. I relaxed and took my notes, thinking this conference had the air of two close friends sitting in a cafe catching up on the day's events.

Months and many meetings had passed since Hammal's spine-chilling introduction. I could still feel the reverberations in the earth. But the initial imperatives had been met; the urgency of his arrival had been established. This accomplished, Hammal could now calmly and deliberately pace his information. The work had already begun and would continue.

"Dearest Julia, angels are messengers of the spiritual realm that bring light, truth, goodness and knowledge of the heart and soul—but there is really no *one* individual angel," said Hammal answering a question I had pondered for some time.

"There are earth angels and cosmic angels. The archangels connect earth angels to the cosmic angels, but all are part of a universal energy flow that ultimately emanates from the Universal Soul," he explained.

"The angelic force is complex," Hammal began to elaborate. "It is directed positive energy within which are many integrated energies. As I mentioned earlier, there are at least 20,000 separating forces that we could touch upon, and countless more. You will understand this better after we discuss the spherical forces. For now, know that we are basically channels, guides to different kinds of knowledge.

"You could say we act as buffers, or messengers, between two worlds, or many worlds, depending on the need.

"Angels perform constant works of good will. We offer protection through our love, speaking only through prayer. Our works are not of our own making, but are universal transmissions from higher states. If asked properly for assistance, with consideration and with respect to your needs, we will help."

The surrounding light had taken on a warm, rosy shade of pink. I wondered if nearby angels had gathered to listen.

"Angels who physically walk the earth in order to help appear as individuals," Hammal disclosed. "Viewed in the human aspect, they *are* individuals."

I was fascinated...."Am I an angel?" I whispered half hoping he wouldn't hear.

"Dearest Julia, yes, you are an angel," Hammal said gently.

I knew it, I really knew it. I'd suspected for a long time, but inside I really knew. I tried not to breathe, afraid I'd wake up and find out I was dreaming.

"Is Havah an angel?"

"Yes, Havah is an angel."

If anyone in the world was an angel it would have to be my dearest Havah.

"Is my mother an angel?"

"Your mother is an alpha angel, working in a beta capacity. She doesn't like to have more than one thing at a time on her mind."

I didn't know what that meant, but I was happy to know that she was an angel.

"Havah's father, is he an angel?"

"Yes, he is an alpha angel."

I went through the names of everyone near and dear to me. I found that one person I knew was on the way to becoming an angel. And I learned my friend Leah, who possessed great powers, was a beta angel since she had shut down her cosmic extensions. Once she reopened the extensions, she would again attain alpha status.

"Is Nikki an angel?" I was talking about my gentle giant, my exquisite poodle, whose face always reflected my joy and pain.

"Yes, Nikki is an angel. Many of your pets are angels. They offer you protection on many planes. Samba now sits in your aura and Baba came to this earth only to be with you. He had finished up his human cycle of reincarnations."

Samba had been a fierce, cocoa-colored Tonkinese cat (a cross between a Burmese and Siamese), a matriarch who never left my side except when she would drape herself around my shoulders or scoot under the covers to keep her lean, elegant, muscular body warm. When she died, I mourned her more than any human I knew. Hammal confided that she had been my mother in another life in another universe.

Baba (Ba-ba') was an exquisite seal point Himalayan, big-boned, regal, gentle, sweet and strong. It took time before I could name him. After some days the name came...Baba...it just came and it was his name. I didn't know what it meant, but the sound rang true.

Baba was his name all right. A week or so later, I checked the dictionary to find that "ba" was the Egyptian word for "spirit of the dead returned" and Baba meant beloved or dear one in East India. So when Hammal told me that I had known Baba in India, and had dearly loved and befriended him when he was a young prince, everything fell into place. I remember telling the man I was dating at the time that if Baba were human, he would have some major competition.

I will love you both forever, my Samba and Baba.

"So what is an angel, really?" I asked, recovering from my private excursion.

"An angel is one who belongs to a complex force of positive energy, a spirit of true goodness," Hammal replied. "One who has the ability to tune into universal direction, allowing his or her direction to join with universal direction. Energy flows to and from an angel—but it is more than that— the flow is a *totality*.

"Like a waterfall, angelic beings live in total prayer, in a *state of connection*, whereby light and goodwill flow to and through them as they offer their energy into higher being."

Hammal paused to let this settle.

"At this time, approximately 3% of all of the individuals on earth are alpha (actual) angels, he continued. "This may seem like a small number, but you must understand that the earth is not a place of ultimate spirituality."

I thought, there are almost six billion people on the earth. What is 3% of six billion? That's a lot of alpha angels considering most people don't think that angels walk the earth.

"An alpha angel possesses a vast amount of knowledge gleaned from many, many lifetimes throughout the galaxies, and becomes aware of this knowledge through his or her good works," he went on.

"If you are an angel of this order, you are able to transcend your physical form and go elsewhere in the universe to protect. You may take on a physical or a nonphysical form, or both simultaneously. This means you have cosmic extensions and can extend or project your energy or force throughout the universe while still in a physical form on earth."

"Am I this kind of angel?" I questioned.

"Yes, Julia, you work even while you sleep and are doing much more than you are aware of."

Hammal's reference here was to the grieving souls. The pieces would fit into place in a later meeting.

"Samba and Baba are also cosmic angels. They came to help, protect and teach you in a physical form that could be accepted in this solar system. Many cats and other animals are angels."

"What about beta angels," I asked. "Are there many on the earth?"

"Everyone on the earth has the *capacity* to become a beta angel, which is an individual who lives for more than him or herself. Everyone can be an angelic soul and connect to the energies of the angelic forces through prayer. In this way you work for the greater good, addressing the needs of others along with your own. At present, about 22% of all individuals on the earth are beta angels.

"This does not mean that as a beta angel you are doing angelic work, but it does mean that you are able to be *touched* by the angels. You can tune into the vibration of the angelic force and receive gifts from the angels through your positive attitudes, actions and direction.

In case you were wondering, an individual can be an alpha and a beta angel at the same time.

I thought back to Hammal's first message, "Eight is peace on earth, when you have learned and you know." I still didn't know what the number meant, but I was beginning to see how there could be peace.

"All souls *must* aspire to be angels," Hammal emphasized, "for this is the plan of the universe. All souls on the earth must become beta angels since no one can leave the earth's cycle of reincarnations unless a certain stage of beta evolvement has been attained. Becoming an alpha angel, however, requires much selfless good work and much love, compassion and kindness.

"Your mother has been an alpha angel. But in this life she has chosen not to work throughout the universe. Your friend Leah has the ability to be an alpha angel and may choose to reopen her cosmic extensions in this lifetime."

"Are alpha and beta angels considered earth angels?" I asked, needing further clarification.

"Not necessarily, Julia. To be an earth angel you must have been born *of* the earth—the earth must have been the birthplace of your *soul*. Many angels who work with, and on, the earth have been born in other parts of the cosmos. You, Julia, are a cosmic angel.

"When I told you earlier that it is I who marshals the Cosmic Angelic Force on your behalf, I meant exactly that. You and I, Mantra, Jake, Farrse, Icail and the others are part of the same Cosmic Angelic Force. We are all known to you and will do the work that you are not allowed to do, or cannot do, in your present physical form.

"Your mother was born not of this earth either. She comes from another part of the cosmos. But she is very comfortable here since her birth planet is very much like the earth—a place where each individual works out his or her life alone in a little box, communicating mentally. It is very fortunate when they have someone to share it with."

Hammal allowed me to think this over before he continued.

"Earth angels," he went on, "may choose to remain on the earth plane to work in physical or nonphysical form. They may choose to work in greater silence with individuals on the earth without cosmic extensions and still be alpha angels."

Confused by this information, I asked, "What do you mean 'choose to work in greater silence with individuals on earth'?"

"Dearest Julia, I am describing the nonphysical *guardian* angels who work with individual, embodied souls and silently offer their light (knowledge), protection and love. This work and form is of their own choosing. Even without cosmic extensions, earth born angels, working in this capacity, are alpha angels.

"Lenore, your late teacher, was an embodied earth angel whose positive energy extends far out into the cosmos. Send her your love forever, Julia—she is a great soul who is with you now, as are 108 teachers and protectors, working directly with you in your aura. And these are connected to many more who come and go as needed." Hammal had unfolded more of the hierarchy.

"Your beloved friend Havah is a cosmic angel and part of your soul. She has worked with you and protected you in many of your lives on earth." The rosy glow grew brighter.

The intricacies of the angelic functions were complex, but the structure was simply pure love that forever emanated from the Universal Soul. "My orders come from the Infinite which is Infinite," Hammal told me one day, "so high that even I have no idea where they originate."

The thought that each and everyone on the earth was on the way to becoming an angel, becoming linked with a place so high, gave peace to my soul.

I thought of the lost souls, and searched for a thread to unravel the reasons for "confused knowledge." I knew many pieces of the puzzle were still missing, but took great comfort in knowing that Hammal and the Cosmic Angelic Force had arrived.

"All of mankind, have angelic forces within, and they are gained through ultimate and everlasting good work." Hammal Cahone

II
The Structure of
the Universe

Chapter 5
Some Questions Answered

Who am I? Where do I come from? What is life?

My questions never ended, but getting direct answers when I wanted them wasn't all that easy. Hammal would patiently clarify confusions regarding my personal life with great tact and concern. But more times than not, my abstract queries would be put off with "write your questions down and we'll discuss them at the next meeting."

So I would diligently write and present my probes only to hear that the "airwaves" held too much static, the planets were misaligned, or the balance wasn't right for my particular questions.

Obstacles seemed endless. Hammal had his agenda and set the way in which he wanted his information presented. So when I was given leeway, I tried to include every question I could think of.

The following account is from one of the rare meetings in which my esoteric ponderings would be met with solid responses. Hammal convened the conference out of the blue on a Saturday morning, announcing that I could read my questions. I scurried for my note-pad, pen and growing list of inquiries, hoping that I could glean a few gems.

"Who am I?" I asked, starting at square one.

"You are an infinite being," replied Hammal. "You are completely derived of infinite beings. All humanity is derived of infinite beings. This answer should, and could, teach you of the simple structure of the universe."

The answer was an enigma, but I was elated. "Just write Julia. Think about it later," I told myself. "You've got your foot in the door." I settled down to pen the precious notes that I would relish in my own good time.

"Where do I come from?"

Hammal echoed my second question, then responded instantly, "This you will have to find out for yourself. There isn't just one answer. As *energy,* we all come from one place, but as characters, we come from many."

I thought of the concept of the One and the outpouring of the All—something I had recently read. Was this the energy he meant?

"As energy and force, the human race is working out its dreams—each person his or her own dream, so that each might find a place of comfort where each can listen to the Universe as a totality," Hammal continued in his poetic angel-speak.

"It is important to think in universal terms," he empha- sized. "Universes are merely different forms of direction. A universe is an episode in which something is fulfilled—a role known as karma has to be completed.

"Each universe has its own character, and within each universe is a form that must be followed. Every universe has a pattern for living. There is a method for every act, a method for every form—a method for existence. This is the universal pattern."

"So..." I wondered, "Am I a universe?"

Hammal seemed to read my mind. "A universe can be one person's universe, one person's realm," he explained. "One universe is the same as any other—smaller or larger does not exist; in this context, greatness or lesserness is nonexistent. The *basic rules of order* are the same. The goal of one universe is the goal of all, or the Ultimate Universe. In reference to weights and measures everything is ultimately the same."

Everything seemed to fit snugly with something I had heard before. But it was still too abstract. I was looking for something more concrete. The thought that I might be expecting too much from an angel occurred to me. After all, Hammal was bringing light from the spiritual realm.

"What is life?" I asked, half expecting to hear something about a river.

"Life as we know it on this earth is a *direction*." Hammal responded.

In future conferences, I would become very accustomed to the word direction. It was crucial to Hammal's mission.

"Direction," he explained, "is a role that you play in order to develop your soul." When you come into this life, you are given certain gifts that will aid in your predetermined direction. When you use your gifts, certain lessons are encountered whereby your soul learns through pain," Hammal expounded.

"So," I thought, "we all know what we are getting into *before* we are born. We all *agree* to certain terms, come through a prescribed person or family to either remain with them or continue on in some other way as we play out our part in a scripted drama.

"All of life *is* a stage," I mused, "a theatrical stage and a stage of learning. We are all at a certain stage on a stage." I entertained myself with the wordplay while jotting myself an explicit note to ask about learning through pain.

The "gifts," I ascertained, were not just talents, but included the circumstances, situations, other souls, elements and issues each of us confronts while following our direction.

In another conference, I actually did hear the 64 million dollar explanation—life is a river. But with all of the blanks filled in, the answer was fascinating.

"What is the body?" I asked, thinking that a more down-to-earth question would demand a more concrete explanation.

"Your body is the reflection of your soul. It is the vehicle in which your soul works out its predetermined role," Hammal's reply was short and direct, but I needed more. So he continued.

"You can also think of your body as the door through which you enter to exist *with* the earth," he said. "It allows you to become one with the planet. Your body is a system that is used within the earth's resources. Perhaps it's an obvious fact, but you take on a *physical* body to connect with the *physical* earth. Other universes are different.

"With your body, you take in your life's *breath*. When you are in tune with your breath and your direction, you can find peace and tranquility on the earth. Many who find it difficult to accept what the earth has to offer find it difficult to inhale.

"Sensations are derived through your body—feeling and dealing with matters of the heart are big factors on the earth. Many other universes do not deal with sensations at all.

"Through your physical body, you learn pain. One of your first lessons in life is to learn to *feel*. Fire, air, water and the elements of the earth that make up your body and make the earth function are some of your teachers.

"Your body is a boundary. Everything within the existence of the earth has boundaries. Your heart is a boundary within the boundary of your body. Boundaries are also lessons.

"Ultimately, you will be able to go beyond the boundaries of your existence. But you must be true to yourself (your soul) in all situations," Hammal continued. "In this way, each lesson you encounter in your body reaffirms your soul's direction and validity.

"To aid in the growth of your soul, you are given what you need both prior to and during your life or stay here on the earth—these are your gifts. However once your soul has touched the earth you cannot leave until your total commitment has been fulfilled.

Your *ultimate goal* is freedom earned through self-respect, self-love, self-kindness and self-appreciation—all of which are the same. Through this, love, respect, knowledge, kindness and appreciation is gained for all humanity."

As Hammal went on, I found myself thinking that love and respect for all is an abstraction humanity has considered in its highest moments. But how many of us actually cultivate self-love or are taught to appreciate ourselves as special souls, or to value and respect ourselves as individuals? I wondered, since it seemed to me that most of us confuse self-appreciation with selfishness.

"Each lesson you are given," Hammal elaborated, "is given with *freedom* as the ultimate goal—freedom from the needs and wants of the earth. With this freedom comes the ability to travel through the cosmos and on to other worlds."

I took a deep breath, trying to imagine the soaring cosmic flight of freedom Hammal was describing.

"This direction to ultimate freedom can be accomplished through the use of prayer and positive thought, among other ways. Many roads, many roles lead to self-awareness." Hammal had answered my question to his satisfaction.

Feeling a bit daring and not terribly angelic, I asked, "How does sex fit into the picture?"

"Sex teaches you about the earth by dealing with another human form outside of your body. Like breathing, sex will ultimately make you feel at one with the universe. Both are teachers of the earth outside of your individual self. Both are lessons in balance. Sex and breath are two different doorways to the universe and the understanding of yourself. They are roads to self-awareness.

"When you include love and kindness, sex is adult play. Sexual dysfunction or sexual abuse is an inability to deal with another human being."

"What *is* the soul?" I asked quickly, sensing I was running out of time.

"Your soul is your direction," Hammal responded. "Your soul is love, and the depth of your love. It is a universe of love so pure and clear that you *see* because you love. A universe unto itself—your soul is your *truth of understanding.*

"Another enigma," I thought. But after contemplating the explanation, I saw that it wasn't.

"Souls are powerful," he went on. "They are truth given virtue through appreciation. Within your soul is the height of your loving compassion, and love is the touching of souls."

As he spoke, I felt at one with the angels. I sensed that I was touching every soul, every thread of light woven into the fabric of the Universe. It was an at-oneness I experienced in deep meditation and at the height of sexual ecstasy. I knew, instantly, what Hammal was talking about. I had left the boundaries of my body.

Hammal suggested that we take a break and meet again later in the day.

It was late evening before we could continue. The air had cleared as the tides that pulled twilight into night resolved.

Hammal greeted me, ready to answer my questions, so I wasted no time in getting down to business.

"Tell me about the earth and the universal plan," I asked, fishing for insight into the seven circles.

Hammal began his story. "At one time all the dry land of the earth was one mass that existed separately from the oceans. But humanity created destructive forces—negative energies that were absorbed into the earth. This negativity, internalized by the earth, continued to build until the earth could no longer tolerate the pressure; the earth was torn to pieces by the negativity humankind created.

"After the eruption, the destructive forces dissipated and the positive fields again attracted the core. So while the *core* came together, the land could *not*. Each time the earth is destroyed, the situation worsens, and the "faults" become more tenuous.

"It is a bad signal when the land starts breaking up in an attempt to release the negativity, like the earthquakes, surprise erosions, and the so-called acts of nature that the earth is experiencing at this time." He was reminding me of the work at hand.

I thought of remnants of highly advanced civilizations, the unresolved archeological finds that our scientists couldn't place into historical context. Are these leftover evidence of earlier earths? Later when Hammal would discuss the Bible he would point out verses that were vestiges of former Bibles.

Then Hammal volunteered information I thought was beyond the scope of my question. But looking back, I realize that his words struck the heart of it. "You should become aware of the fact that the earth is neither a place of ultimate power nor of ultimate spirituality," he said. "It is simply a place to gain knowledge through love and compassion.

"When you come to the earth, you make a commitment with the core (the soul) of the earth to learn power through the thinking mind and learn love through debt—you owe and pay, are owed to and are paid. This is the premise on which earth was created—it is the *original* concept, and a very workable situation for a *directed* soul. Once this is learned, your soul can continue on.

"However, since debt is universal, the decision was made to give all souls a chance on the earth, many of which do not have direction. Lack of direction is the worst. Add freedom of choice to lack of direction and, in most souls, utter confusion is created. Added to this, the grieving souls are multiplying the pain tenfold."

Hammal had just flashed a light on how a soul could be lost through careless knowledge. Another clue.

Having completed his answer, he awaited my next question.

"You stated that the earth was throwing off the entire solar system and beyond," I said. "What is beyond?"

With this, Hammal began to sketch the unfathomable Superstructure. He recounted 18 earths, 18^2 solar systems, 18^4 universes, 18^8 cosmos, 18^{16} eternities, 18^{32} finities and 18^{64} infinities.

I observed that everything became the number *nine*. 1+8=9, 18x18=324 which is 3+2+4=9. I remembered Hammal had said "Infinity is nine," and reasoned that anything beyond the earth, to us on the earth, *was* Infinity.

I looked at the words finities, infinities, cosmos and eternities and thought how frustrating it must be for a cosmic being to attempt an explanation of the Superstructure with our limited concepts. The plural form of cosmos was nonexistent, and finity wasn't a place—a vocabulary stuck in an ancient concept of heaven and earth. I pictured the four mountains that supported the dome of heaven over the earth—a widely accepted belief not all that long ago.

"All earths have a similar physical structure," Hammal was speaking. Being in the 16th Universe, they are near the lowest of the solar systems and are heavier and down to basics.

"Mythological beings such as Pegasus exist in the Fifth Cosmic Universe.

"In the Fourth Solar System, a place called Sardonia exists as a place for cleansing and strengthening.

"Every place has its own reason or direction for being. And each place will continue to repeat itself, as the earth is continually reborn, until the pattern no longer is needed.

"The inhabitants of each place—those who are there to learn from it—must follow the rules and comfortably flow within the structure, listening to the nature of each place.

"Direction (the things that you should be doing) comes in thought forms. If you are to follow a certain direction and you do not go with it, then you go against yourself," he continued.

"In order to learn from the earth, you must follow the rules. To follow the rules, you must be directed or disciplined. If you do not have paying and reaping and building and balancing continually on your mind, you will fall apart mentally and physically. This is what is happening on the earth today."

Not exactly the answer I had hoped for. Hammal had diverted my train of thought back to the grieving souls. But I didn't press for more information. For now, I had more than enough to think about. Hammal brought the meeting to a close, and we agreed to meet the following day.

I thought of the meaning of direction, reread my notes and added debt to my growing list of topics.

Chapter 6
Currents and Vibrations

"Dearest Julia, As I contact you from the cosmos, forces are set in motion; likewise, your vibrations are traveling throughout the universe. We are each part of a unity." Hammal Cahone

The rainy season was upon Miami. Like the monsoons in India, we were having real wadi washes almost daily. Lightening cracked, thunder rolled, the streets flooded and traffic snarled along with the frustrated drivers. It was Friday. I had spent most of the day cozy and dry, working on a new 14-karat gold horoscope series based on the female form.

I love the intense concentration that allows me to transcend time and tap into the collective energy of certain artists when I create jewelry. I absorb the vibrations of different time periods and societies, especially ancient Egypt or the Mayan culture. The pieces come to me almost like automatic handwriting.

A productive day gently merged into a pleasant and noticeably cooler night—the rain had stopped; crickets, palmetto bugs, toads and frogs were out splashing, scooting and singing in the clear, sweet, wet, earthy air.

Satisfied with my efforts, I sat down to savor an icy slice of watermelon, surrounded by the pleading eyes of my poodle trio, Nikki, Tina and Aaron, and my fruit-aholic Yorkie Hairy. I made a feeble attempt at the lion's share, but as usual they won. It was half for me and half for them, plus dish washing privileges.

I placed the pendant I had finished that afternoon on the table—Cancer the Crab—the sun sign I had designed with Havah in mind. The gold, Lalique-like, lyric figure shimmered under the light. Obviously a nude female figure, perched on the moon—at least that's how it appeared at first casual glance. But closer scrutiny revealed the moon, fashioned in filigree, defined the large crab claws while the woman's arms and flowing hair extended into the smaller claws—a fascinating piece.

I couldn't wait to tell Havah her piece was ready. But she was out of town for the weekend. So I settled down to relax, about to turn on the TV, when Hammal arrived.

Almost immediately I found myself out in space without an anchor. It was the place where I was instantly transported whenever Hammal convened what he called "A Conference on Infinity"—talks and lectures that focused on the earth, humanity and the cosmic picture.

Totally comfortable in the vast inky expanse, with only Hammal's velvet voice to guide me, I could expand myself in all directions and travel on his words.

"Dearest Julia, as I contact you from the cosmos, forces are set in motion; likewise, your vibrations are traveling throughout the universe—we are each part of a unity," he began.

"Vibrations drive us and give us our energy. They make up the currents on which we all exist. Every vibration in every universe affects the currents that affect us all." He began to unfold a totally new subject.

"Have you ever watched a rubber band as it bounces back when you pluck it?" he asked.

I wanted to understand everything Hammal was saying.

So I found a rubber band, stretched it around my thumb and forefinger, and plucked it to watch the movement

"This is how a vibration moves," he said. "Each of us sends out vibrations like a rubber band. The vibrations move with the same rhythm, but circularly and very, very quickly, as a spherical force, in unending vibrations.

"Continuous waves of expression emanate from every presence in this way. They touch every other object, every organism, with or without a body—forever."

He paused to allow me to absorb the concept.

Seated on my cushion of air in boundless space, I could hear the din of billions upon billions of rubber bands—messages humming, vibrations moving over the airwaves. I couldn't make out what was being said, but the air was seething with activity—like a social gathering of all the crickets, frogs and beetles in the universe after a rain.

"The spherical movements send reflexes into action that are similar to throwing a ball," Hammal continued. "Once tossed, the ball is automatically returned to the pitcher."

"Consciously and unconsciously, we are all continually tossing and catching an infinite number of balls, ceaselessly creating an endless stream of vibrations. And when even *one* ball is out of sync, we *feel* it."

The blue-black expanse came alive with beads of energy moving so quickly that they blurred into colored threads, swirling over, under, around and through me. I could now see as well as hear the incessant activity pulsing throughout the universe and beyond.

"The vibration of a physical movement travels so quickly that it can circle the earth once in a second," Hammal elaborated. "On its journey, a vibration combines with other vibrations. If the vibration being sent is positive and combines with another positive vibration, the positive vibration is amplified. If the amplified vibration is joined by a negative vibration, the total vibration is weakened." Simple plus and minus math, I noted.

"Every movement, even a hand movement, comes back to you in this way. It may not return in its identical form or motion, but it does come back with its original intent—the circular movement, or spherical force, picking up velocity by the weight of its movement."

He waited for a minute to make sure that I was following him, then continued.

"A vibration instigated with negative intent will be, unhappily, picked up by other individuals and eventually relay an unpleasant vibration to the sender. If it joins with other negative vibrations on its journey, it can devastate the sender, depending on the weight of its original intent."

As Hammal spoke, I realized more than simple math was involved. He was now talking velocity and weight.

"There are times when you might feel edgy and don't know why," Hammal went on. "Other times you may sense an overwhelming presence of love and well-being. And everyone has felt an itch with no apparent cause. You are sensing vibrations."

He went on to explain that vibrations join other vibrations to form *currents* of energy. And as he spoke, I saw the spherically swirling beaded threads merge into brilliant ribbons of light.

"Currents have no measured time sequence. They only pull," he explained. "And it is on these currents that souls and light travel—like you do when you design a piece of jewelry, Julia."

Swept along on a multicolored current, I could feel the power of the movement, hear the hum of the collective reverberations, and see other vibrations flash by. I thought about magnets. They create streams of energy that pull without regard to time.

Hammal stepped in to take my image a step farther. "Imagine a tug-of-war rope attached to everything in the universe," he said. "What you need is pulled in toward you. As an individual soul, you act as a *current* of exchange within the spherical forces surrounding you."

My mind soared off on a tangent. I considered the possibility of consciously manipulating a magnetic current to draw all the things I wanted into my life. I visualized the things I needed, and I tugged on the rope.

The image was powerful. A huge door had opened and I was inundated by light flying out in all directions, as if I had opened a magical box filled with positive energy. Swept on a current of thought, I had traveled light years away in a microsecond.

I could hear Hammal's voice faintly in the distance, saying, "Everyone on the earth has a vibration that touches everyone else on the planet, even if you have never met. Each vibration moves throughout the earth to make up a part of every other organism."

As I traveled back, Hammal's voice became louder. "Much more is touching you than you would ever begin to suspect," he said. "When an individual body dies on the earth, a living vibration is lost, and the loss of this vibration influences everyone on the earth.

"The death of a two-year-old child in the mountains of Tibet affects each individual at least 1/3 of one percent; a birth will set up new vibrations that will touch you in the same way.

"If you know the soul who is being born or is leaving, the impact of their vibration increases according to the strength of the individual that is going or coming. If you have known the soul in a past life or lives, but not in this one, his or her vibrations will still actually touch you," he emphasized.

"When disasters occur and many souls leave their bodies in shock and pain—even if the disaster occurs halfway around the globe—we all feel the heaviness in the air," he went on.

"The heaviness you feel is the weight of the pained souls who, through shock, have lost their direction—souls that may or may not be in their bodies."

Another allusion to the grieving souls. I thought of the recent air disasters we had been experiencing. Our entire outlook for the earth, our personal attitudes, our fears, our hopes and our collective futures are all being affected.

Hammal interrupted my thoughts to announce that we would stop to let the vibration of this conference settle and we'd pick up where we left off at our next meeting. With that, he instantly departed.

I slept soundly, comfortably carried on currents all night. I awoke early the next morning, went to the studio where I added some touches to a portrait I had begun, taught my Saturday students about the energy forces inherent in the structure of a Cezanne landscape, and returned home.

Sometimes days and weeks came and went between meetings. So I was surprised when Hammal reappeared the same night to announce that the air was still clear for the incoming topic. I was delighted that the information was coming in so quickly and that he was wasting no time.

"Thought vibrations are much more powerful than physical vibrations," he continued where he had left off. "A physical attack may leave visible wounds but does not often have the power of thought—thoughts invade much more deeply.

"The onslaught of a thought vibration is eight times stronger than a physical beating—and lasts eight times longer." The number eight was significant.

"Thought vibrations travel timelessly, and so quickly, that as soon as you think them, they are done. To be more specific, they are actually done *before* you think them. Conscious thought is actually an afterthought—a reflection of the original thought that follows as old news," he elaborated.

"Negative thoughts effect many things, including wars. When a war has ended, it takes approximately eight years for one who has fought in a war to experience true joy and light. Momentary joys may be experienced, but true joy that touches truth and light is impossible.

"Even those who were not in the actual fighting have suffered from the onslaught of vibrations. Fear, pain, and the like will remain as a spot on each. This, too, will take eight years to heal and clear."

When Hammal delivered a lecture on infinity, my mind would drift in and out. I would go from the message at hand to the questions remaining. This meeting was no different, and I was off and thinking.

I had recently learned that it took "eight" to set a new vibration and begin on a new road. The concept fit.

My thoughts wandered to the earth in the seventh circle and Hammal's riddle: *There is no eight on earth.* How could this be if it took eight years to recover from a major war and eight days, hours or whatever, to recover from a thought vibration?

Hammal had said that mankind had misunderstood the meaning of the circles. I wondered if the notion of eight was similar to a musical octave where eight is actually the first number of the next round.

Do-re-me-fa-sol-la-ti-do is the musical scale. *Do* is one, *re* is two, *me* is three, *fa* is four, *sol* is five, *la* is six, *ti* is seven, and *do* finishes the octave. But *"do"* is not really eight when you are to <u>continue</u> on. It is, rather, the first note of the next octave—or the first level of the next circle or round. The concept held.

Hammal nodded and smiled—he had read my thoughts. And I had unlocked another piece of the puzzle. What fun it was to talk to angels, I thought. No words were exchanged about the number. But I had my answer, and Hammal continued to deliver his scheduled information without a break in pace.

"Vibrations are not merely feelings," he said. They are a pre-understanding or experience of something. Most sensitivity is based on this knowledge.

"Currents come from everywhere. They are our form of association. But individual currents differ—some are more vital than others since some are closer to your soul.

"A higher level of communication brings with it greater responsibility; the more you 'hear' the greater your accountability to your soul *(your direction)* and the greater the rewards gained. If channels have previously opened for you, you will have a certain clarity and working knowledge of existence," he went on.

I then, truly knew that there had been channels opened for me, things that I innately comprehended, but couldn't yet touch.

"Currents are like debts to be paid," he elaborated. "Since you know there is something to be gained by following the current, you must follow it. Once a door is opened it can *never* be shut. Just as a hurt can never be made up, a current can only be set aside for a time. Forgetting would be a lie."

Hammal was implying something about the grieving souls and my responsibility to them—something not yet revealed. Was he attempting to unfold information about the structure of the universe in order to prepare me? I would learn that this was exactly what he was doing.

"When you feel the pull of a current, you are *responsible* to make some kind of commitment to it in order to fulfill your own life. This can be a most beautiful, fulfilling experience," he continued.

I felt the pull. I definitely felt the pull.

"Much greater than we can imagine, everything has its own current. The pull of the currents has to do with the tug and the pull of the universe. They have nothing to do with balance, but are related to resolution, to learning and to commitment. Those with greater vision have earned their vision by listening for more responsibility."

I felt the responsibility of an unspoken commitment.

"When you ride a current you are tied into the things that you *need* or the things that you can *help*. You will not usually feel the pull of a current that doesn't go along with the tides of your own nature. This is why certain people attract, and are attracted to, similar things."

As Hammal spoke, I knew I was to be very instrumental to the grieving souls. But what was it that I was to do? What would unfold my karmic path?

"The strengths of the currents might cause you to go completely inside of yourself or totally outside of yourself depending on your needs. Working or riding a current might simply mean entering into a relationship of compassion without words," Hammal continued to unfold his message.

"Every planet in the universe has its own currents and vibrations that describe its responsibility to the universe. Some universes relate more to each other, just as individuals do.

"Unlike the earth, some planets associate with each other in a manner that is based on unifying a current, as do two or more people who choose to work together for a higher purpose. The dual or combined responsibility creates a combination of power for which the accountability is vast."

Again I heard the whisper of the lost souls.

"The whole universe works in this way: what you need is *pulled in* through the spherical forces around you. Currents run through every pore, but some people close off. You can accept as much as you are able.

What was it that I was to accept? I knew there was more.

He was about to end his missive, when he added, "If someone you know suffers a loss, take care *not* to send sad vibrations to that person or you will add to the weight and pain they are carrying. Sorrow is not a high vibration. If you send your sadness, you will send more weight and sorrow. Just send your understanding and love.

"It is also important for you to know that every breath from every creature is your own breath. Each of us is made up of the vibrations I have spoken of; the vibrations of each reflect in the lives of us all. Remember that every soul is a part of your soul. Everything that happens to you, happens to everyone of us.

"You and every other soul on earth have a great part in constructing and developing the universe. Everything, including the earth, is continually in the process of becoming. You are right now and forever creating the universe and molding it into what it is and into what it will be.

"Every new thought-form you create, one little object or movement, sends out a vibration that indelibly imprints *infinitely,* not only on this earth's surface but continuously, throughout the Superstructure, throughout time."

This stated, the conference ended. Nothing, as yet, was spelled out...only whispered.

Chapter 7

The Spherical Forces: Links to the Light

"When the spherical forces are clear and properly aligned, one can travel on the light..." Hammal Cahone

For most of my adult life, I thought of my physical body as a visible vehicle, like a bus or a car, that my soul animated for the purpose of acting out my karmic role. When my life on earth was complete, I felt that I would leave my old model behind while my soul, with its precious lessons learned, voyaged to the Light, made a U-turn with another "to do" list and reincarnated into another vehicle.

While on the earth plane, I figured I could take a few astral side trips to check on friends, resolve some questions, or check out some sights when a physical vacation was out of the question.

This simplistic view was fine as far as it went. But Hammal had already extended my concept of infinity in his conference on vibrations and currents. Now, as the sun settled into a sultry, subtropical Sunday evening, he would reveal much more. He would show me how the door to the first level of the next circle could be opened and how I could travel throughout the cosmos while still in a physical body.

"Your physical body is *energy,*" Hammal said, "energy that is linked to the Infinite by the spherical forces.

"The spherical forces are interpenetrations of the auras.

"View yourself as energy in the center of energy. See yourself as part of a whole system of energy—part of a package, or compression, that lines up against interior walls made solely of *thought*—*w*all, upon wall, upon wall of thought, ad infinitum. These walls of thought surround each and every individual.

"The movement of the spherical forces is a double directed movement that goes counterclockwise as it begins, but it goes clockwise, also becoming its opposite."

I pictured my physical body as dense, compacted energy. Surrounding it, I visualized a spherical envelope of less dense energy that was surrounded by another envelope of finer energy, visualizing envelopes that became finer and finer and finer still, moving onward and outward, whirring throughout infinity. The envelopes on the outermost limits whirred the fastest.

"Creative thought drives the entire spherical force," Hammal continued. "Greater or lesser energy is created by greater or lesser understanding." He paused so that I could get my bearings.

I saw the whirring energy envelopes being fed by thought, energy envelopes that *were* thought—layer upon layer of creative thought that linked to higher and higher knowledge, truth and light.

I stopped mid-visualization. If my body is energy surrounded by energy that continues to infinity, and that energy is thought, then my body is, no more or less, dense thought. This opened up a world of possibilities.

Satisfied that I had gotten the picture, Hammal continued. "Simplified, directed and disciplined thought generates greater or lesser spherical force," he said. "Most often, however, the walls (the thoughts) repress or depress the outer regions of cosmic energy, inhibiting new thought."

He paused again.

I considered that it would be difficult to move through a dense fog quickly or accelerate my pace if my vision was limited. Sunlight, however, would burn off the mist and allow me to know and see where I was going; if I had a good idea of where I was going, a good sense of direction, then I could run, almost fly. It was the same with thought—clear, simple thought with a *direction* made the spherical forces speed up.

I went on to picture a child trying to learn phonics. I saw the walls of thought, surrounding the child, slowed down by confusion. But once the child knew how to maneuver within the new framework of sounds, had learned the words and mastered the direction, the energy surrounding the child sped up. Reading then opened up more and more worlds of creative thought and energy.

Likewise, each new lesson learned on the earth, relative to an individual's path, opens up new channels of knowledge enabling him or her to reach farther and farther into "creation," deeper and deeper into the cosmos, merging the individual's whirring energy closer and closer to the all-encompassing Light.

Seeing that I had caught up with the incoming material, Hammal continued, "The universal movement of the spherical forces is made up partly of *soul energy* which is directed thought (your soul's sense of direction), and *angelic force* which is truth—knowledge and light that comes in with kindness.

"On a physical level, the planes and auras that surround you are the intense vibrations that go throughout *this* solar system. Their ties are deeply rooted in the universe. It is the *planal system* that keeps the earth in its own sphere, aligns the universe and keeps it intact.

"The planal system maintains the balance of positive and negative forces in this universe, keeping the energies from destroying each other. At the same time, it paces the flow of new, incoming cosmic light, which is cosmic information. When the earth is ready and it is time for changes in evolution—as it is now—new knowledge flows through these channels onto the earth."

Hammal continued to unfold the information as simply as possible. "You must understand, Julia, the *space* between planets is not empty but completely fluid and incessantly active with positive and negative energies. The universe is electric and forever in motion. And it is the planal system that holds *everything* together.

"The strongest planal system is the "X," the everlasting perpendicular, the points formed where the spherical forces intersect; light flows through the center point to cleanse the auras.

"Traveling on these routes, the angelic forces are kept in procession and thought-forms, coming from the cosmic universe, are kept in perspective.

"As part of the spherical forces, the new things that are channeled in through these planes enter the chakras in the etheric double and continue on into the physical body."

Hammal continued lecturing while directing me to visually illustrate this new information.

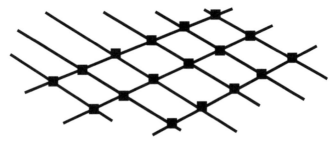

Cross-section of the Planal System located within our Solar System, and the Xs— the everlasting perpendiculars.
The spherical forces do not spin forever in one place, but move in all directions while spinning, like a gyroscope, so the position of the Xs constantly change.

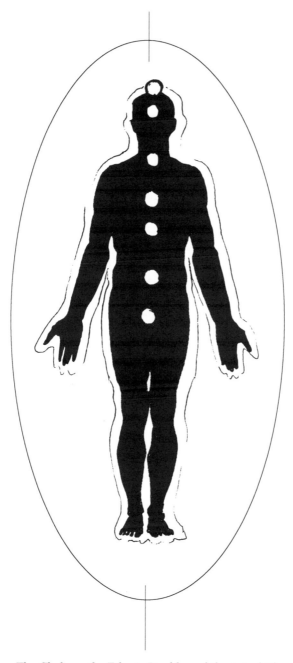

The Chakras, the Etheric Double and the Astral Plane

The Auras

Hammal began to describe, in detail, what he called "the package"—the spherical force that lies closest to the physical body.

"The spherical force that lies closest to the physical body are the auras which are made up of the *etheric double* and the *astral plane*," he said. "Like the earth on its axis, they are aligned by a magnetic pole with positive and negative terminals."

"It is through these planes," he repeated, "that new seeds of knowledge, protection and healing are channeled into our physical bodies."

The Chakras

"The chakras alone," he said, "combine the physical and the cosmic. The more chakras, or other channels, that are open, the more energy you have and the more light you can receive.

"Some individuals have channels open for physical energy, others for mental, and so forth. If no, or low, energy exists, the channels have been shut down and the spherical forces are out of alignment.

"Humanity's concept of the chakras is limited," Hammal went on to note. "No one to date has written about the subject properly. The chakras do align with the pressure points along the meridians in the physical body. But there is more; the *valves in the blood are also tiny chakras*. There is work here for someone to undertake."

The Soul and the Spherical Force

"Your soul exists as part of the spherical force. It moves continuously and very fast. If your soul should leave your body, you would become very nauseated because of the rapid movement.

"Without the weight of your soul, your body lacks substance to hold it down. Without a soul, a body has nothing to respond to. This is why when you lose your soul, you lose yourself."

How interesting, I thought. We on earth have always thought the reverse—that is, if the body no longer can function, the soul leaves.

But what Hammal said made sense. Earlier when asked, "What is the body?" He answered, "...the body is the *reflection* of your soul...the *door* through which you enter to exist with the earth...a system used within the earth's resources that allows you to become one with the planet."

With that in mind, I junked the car simile. Rather than thinking of my body as a piece of machinery animated by my soul, I saw my physical being as a system of thought, a bundle of creative energy, mirroring my *direction* in this particular life.

If things weren't going right for me, this meant that I should look *inward* to my soul to consider my direction and try to connect to the angelic forces for the light, knowledge and answers that my physical situation demanded. The orientation was totally different. And realizing this, I also realized that there was no inward or outward, just connections and interconnections throughout the universe. With that, I flew through the eternal Xs, the doors that formed a channel into the cosmic light.

"Souls gathered together for a singular positive purpose form a unity within the spherical force to become synchronized with the *cosmic* force. Souls aligned in this way are reflected or amplified within the spherical force," Hammal continued.

I thought of more than one instance where individuals have gathered together to prove the power of amplified prayer and bring about healing miracles. At this moment, I touched the power. I was flying and Hammal was still lecturing. I tried, but couldn't stay grounded.

Angels and the Spherical Force

"The angels exist as part of the spherical force—the part of the spherical force that is *thought as appreciation of thought*. The faster the thought of love and thankfulness moves, the greater the appreciation of thought," he said.

Then he added, "As there are different levels of knowledge, there is a hierarchy of angels—the earth angels, archangels and cosmic angels that I have spoken of. When I said the angelic force had 20,000 separating forces that we could touch upon and countless more, I was illustrating the layers upon layers of energies, the endless spherical forces that continue on and on and on throughout the universal superstructure, which in itself is endless.

"And as I have conveyed before, the gifts I bring are directly from the Cosmic Angelic Force. The help that you need is all around you. You just have to listen to your sense of direction—your soul. *Know* that you will be taken care of and link up with the angelic forces—this is prayer. It is the way to live your life as a prayer. It is the doorway to infinity and greater and greater light, knowledge and truth."

Hammal called for a small recess, just enough time for me to fold up my newly-found wings and list the highlights of this conference for my own reference:

1. Man's visible body is composed of *energy.*

2. Man's energy is linked to the Infinite by energy.

3. The energy is creative thought vibrations that are interpenetrations of the auras called the spherical forces.

4. The spherical force is made up partly of soul energy (clear, disciplined, directed thought) and angelic force (thought that is an appreciation of thought—truth that comes in with kindness).

5. Structured much like the solar system, the spherical forces are planes of energy; universal movements that function harmoniously throughout the cosmos. Extending endlessly, the

spherical forces are far greater than the auras seen on the physical plane and much vaster than one could ever imagine.

6. The spherical force that goes throughout *this* solar system are the *planes* and *auras*—intense, strong vibrations. These ties are deeply rooted in the universe and keep the earth in its own sphere.

7. The auric force closest to the *physical* body is comprised of the etheric body and the astral plane. They are aligned by a magnetic pole with positive and negative terminals, like the earth on its axis.

8. The strongest planal system is the X, the everlasting perpendicular. Light flows through its center-point to cleanse the auras. Traveling on these routes, the angelic forces are kept in procession, and thought forms, coming from the cosmic universe, are kept in perspective.

Through these planes new seeds of knowledge, protection and healing are channeled in through the chakras (the etheric double) into the physical body.

9. Uniting us all to the cosmos is creative thought energy. Greater or lesser energy, stimulated by simple, direct, disciplined, understanding thought produces greater or lesser spherical force.

10. When the aligning pole of the auric force closest to the body is centered and the spherical forces are clear and properly aligned, one can travel through these channels on the light throughout the cosmos and infinity.

Hammal then asked if I had any questions.

My head was spinning with this new information. There was no way I could begin to formulate a question.

So Hammal ended by saying, "A clear, balanced aura can amplify a soul through thought and unite it with cosmic consciousness. This new knowledge should account for the alignment of humankind's physical and etheric body with the cosmic energy source."

In the days to come, I thought long and hard about vibrations, currents and spherical forces. For days and weeks, I pictured rubber bands vibrating in circular movements. I saw balls of energy—thought sent spiralling endlessly throughout the cosmos, repeating eternally.

I visualized the atoms, miniature solar systems, spinning within each ball. Traveling forever inward, each atom became its own solar system, ad infinitum.

Traveling outward I viewed the incessant activity within our own solar system—currents moving in, around and through the earth, vibrations being absorbed by each of us and by the earth. I saw how we responded to the infinite balls that touched us, how we tossed them back to the senders—everything locked in endless, ever-expanding motion—the layers of thought-energy, packaged around thought-energy, around thought—spherical forces moving ever outward into infinity meshing and intermeshing—energies forever crisscrossing, ever alive.

I watched highly illuminated thoughts traveling great distances. I noticed how the thoughts that could travel the farthest linked up with the light of greater knowledge. I carefully noted how the shells around each individual could repress thought and restrain an individual on his journey to the light.

I thought of the atomic structure as applied to a physical body—how the body was built of simple cells which were dependent on their atomic structure. I considered how the well-being of the whole body depended on the health of each individual cell, and applied my concept to the universe—wondering to what extent the cosmic body would be injured if the earth is destroyed.

I pictured the lost souls as individual cells who ate away at themselves and who were thus destroying the whole body.

I thought back to the beginning of our relationship when Hammal had announced he was part of a new consciousness coming to humanity that had waited for the right time to present itself. He stated that before he could continue, the grieving souls had to be balanced. Until this was done, they would continue to build negativity and block the light.

He had just explained the mechanics of the problem. I could now understand how the light was being blocked by the imbalance of energies in the spherical forces, the planal system and the eternal Xs. It was now clear that increasing negative electrical currents threw the eternal Xs out of alignment.

It was obvious that the negativity in the spherical forces, combined with excessive negative forces built up into the earth, could create an electrical overload that could shatter the earth into pieces.

I also found that I could easily travel on the light.

And at this moment, I understood that life was indeed a river since no space existed in the universe. Everything was a river of positive and negative energies, currents and vibrations, waves, eddies and spherical forces—forever fluid and infinitely in motion.

I thought of Hammal's cabinet, the six Cosmic Angels and their functions. More pieces of the puzzle were being dropped into my lap. Still, I waited to be told of *my* function.

The Spherical Forces

Chapter 8

Heart, Soul, Universal Soul, Universal Mind

"Dearest Julia, You own your soul. It is yours. It is your positive direction, your love. You do not own your mind, however. The individual mind does not exist." Hammal Cahone

"Well, that's a relief," I laughed. "After last weekend's lectures, I'm glad to know that it's not *my* mind that's in a tailspin."

Hammal laughed. I was always a little surprised and delighted when Hammal appreciated my funnies. Frankly, I don't usually consider angels and joking around in the same breath. But, I've found, angels can be very playful. And Hammal has a great sense of humor.

Once, in the middle of a serious discussion, I asked him: "What is God?" I was informed very frankly that God was much like a clock. "The universe was set in motion and continues on," he explained.

Later, when he excused himself mid-conference, and I asked him where he was going, he simply announced that he was off "to wind the clock."

"Much humor exists in the cosmic universe," he confided one afternoon, "that is, humor with joy and light and love—the kind of humor that holds understanding—as when angels look on the earth and smile to each other in amusement."

"Humor is the *teacher* of love and warmth," Hammal went on, adding with great understanding, "Humor on earth is very important. It is a form of release—a way for humanity to throw off insecurities and doubts. Without humor, pain grows into greater fear—the fewer the doubts, the less the pain and the less the fear."

"Humor is never inappropriate," he whispered. "It fills a vital need and should never be questioned. Without humor, the spirit would die. This would begin the closing of the soul."

"Ridicule is not humor, however," he cautioned, "true humor is never misused."

"The light and love of humor show true compassion; many times, humor has been the only way karmic debts have been fulfilled."

But humor was not this evening's topic. Tonight I was to learn what was mine and what was not mine. Hammal was very direct and focused. I settled down with my pen poised.

"Your soul is yours," he began. "You own your soul. It is your positive direction, your love.

"You own your heart. It belongs to you. Your heart is closely tied to your soul. It is the evolvement of your *individual* soul, its purity and its positive direction.

"All souls are good but some souls have a higher evolvement based on the heart. The greater your heart, the greater your compassion, your light and your love, and the clearer your vision," he elaborated.

"Beyond your individual soul and your individual heart is the Universal Soul. When your soul leaves your body, it goes into a purified state, becoming part of the Universal Soul unless it is a grieving or a lost soul and is unable to continue on.

"You don't own your mind. There is only the Universal Mind—*individual* minds do not exist. Individual minds are receptors of energy, currents and vibrations.

"When you open your mind, you are allowing the knowledge of the universe to filter in to you through the spherical forces. Individual minds are conductors and collectors of energy.

"You do not own your knowledge. Knowledge is a gift that is given to you to embellish or enhance in a positive, creative way.

"Your mind and knowledge have nothing to do with your ego. Your ego is a part of your persona, your individuality, on the earth. If you claim ownership to knowledge it will be destructive to the universe.

"Your will is yours. As a receptor of information, what you *do* with the knowledge you receive is based on your free will.

"Now Julia, please repeat back to me what you understand," Hammal quizzed. "It is vital that you comprehend this information clearly."

I repeated, "There is only One Mind—the Universal Mind. My mind is a receptor of transmissions, a universal conductor and collector of energy—a piece of the Universal Mind. Each individual mind is a creative power that exists *solely* to function as part of the Universal Mind.

"Transmissions from the Universal Mind travel through the spherical forces. The abilities that exist in my mind are totally dependent upon how open my 'receptor' (my mind) is to the knowledge of the universe. I do not own my own mind; my mind has nothing to do with my ego which is part of my existence on the earth.

"I do not own my knowledge. My knowledge is a gift that is given to me so that I can embellish or enhance it with creative thought in a *positive* manner. The second I try to claim ownership for knowledge, it is destructive to our universe.

"My heart, my soul and my will are mine. My heart has everything to do with the evolution of my individual soul. It is united to my soul—my soul being positively directed truth, positive energy focused by my reason for being.

"My will is my freedom of choice; how I exercise my free will, dictates the outcome of my choices."

"This is true," Hammal said and went on to explain. "It is very important that you understand this message very clearly because we are *now* in the midst of a spiritual war—Dark and Light, at this moment, exist *equally* on earth. All must become keenly aware of these duelling energies—the future of your universe depends on it." He paused to allow the impact of this disconcerting truth to settle.

"As this war is being waged, earth minds are receiving higher and higher levels of knowledge due to the movement throughout the universe. The profuse transmissions in Mind-Thought are initiating many, many currents that are intensely vibrating with increasing speed. This is part of the *scheduled* evolution of the universe."

So, I thought, the universe *was* a clock, ticking according to universal plan and humanity was out of sync. Hammal had been joking on the square; he really was here to "wind the clock."

By misinterpreting the incoming transmissions, we were misdirecting our free will to re-configure a preset clockwork into a ticking time bomb.

"To date universal energy has been misunderstood and misinterpreted by humanity," he continued. "The human race has been negatively directing Universal Mind energies, utilizing them with the wrong intent.

"Since all on the earth are so closely tied, the erroneous vibrations have set up currents that, even though incorrect, are being acted upon. Humankind is aware of the energy dichotomies that exist today.

"This energy imbalance must be rebalanced quickly—the *speed* of the incoming Mind-Energy, along with a lost system of values, can cause the earth to destruct right now.

"It is *crucial* that we be pure of heart, soul and intent because so much power is coming to humanity at this time. It is absolutely imperative that we are positive in our thoughts and direction.

"Humanity must be clearer and purer to properly accept this incoming new knowledge. Your *hearts* must guide you because it is though the purity of heart that good works are done.

"If you are wondering why, with all the powerful helpers in the universe, we have come to this. It has to do solely with the human race and its misunderstanding of the heart and the soul which are ultimately the same.

Powerful helpers are always available, but only through *positive* vibrations can you invite them in, for they are the energies of the heart world."

This message was brief but powerful. I pass it on to you.

Chapter 9

The Lifeline from Life to Life

"Dearest Julia, There is a schedule for each and every soul—an ultimate plan." Hammal Cahone

The train rocked rhythmically as it rushed through the clear, crisp early autumn morning.

I was six or seven-years-old and lost in the oversized, over-stuffed drab seat in the drafty coach. I pressed myself into the itchy horsehair upholstery and pulled at my three-quarter length coat, trying cover my bony knees, but the recently purchased, pale blue topper didn't quite reach.

My young mother sat facing me, comfortable in her new beige cashmere. Meticulously outfitted in our very best, we were on our way to Philadelphia to visit Mummy's thin-lipped, domineering older sister.

My mother quietly gazed out through the closed window. Hypnotized by the monotonous rhythm of the wheels, her mind sailed somewhere in the distance.

I surveyed her profile. Framed by the plush collar that crowned her coat, she looked regal. How I ached to be as beautiful as she was when I grew up.

A graphite-like odor permeated the car as the wheels and rails wore at each other, mile after mile, droning their monotonal taunts—clakity-clak, clackity-clack, clackity, clakity...The smell merged with the melange of tobacco, passengers and the tart, dry, heated air to invade our space and mix with my mother's heady floral perfume.

Sleepy from the scents and sounds, I followed her gaze into the miles of tranquil fields and sunlit hills where autumn had already touched the leaves, and tried to counter the occasional sobering chill that swept through the coach whenever the door between the cars was opened.

I took deep breaths and crunched into the corner, hoping the sun would warm my icy knees as it heated the window pane. Yet peacefully scanning the vista I felt like a princess reviewing my realm.

"You are very rich," I heard my Sunday School teacher say. "Your Father owns everything your eyes can see."

If my Father owned everything I saw, then everything is mine, I decided and at that moment, I owned the world.

There are still days when I own the world but I am always overwhelmed by the universe.

My thoughts turned to the time when I had questioned Hammal about the ego and the Universal Mind...

Hammal told me that the Universal Mind belonged to the Superstructure but the ego was the *I* that belonged to the earth. The ego was the persona I adopted *here* and had to go *beyond* so that my mind (my receptor) could be a clear receiver and transmitter of the Universal Mind.

Just as my body was the earthly vehicle of my soul, my ego was the mechanism through which I learned to be open to the Universal Mind and the truth of my being.

I still don't understand why my childhood scrapbook flew open when Hammal had begun to speak or why I wandered on to the Universal Mind from there. Perhaps an empty, fleeting feeling made me seek a crisp, clear, sunny morning in autumn when my mother would be riding with her little daughter on a train. Maybe when Hammal said, "There is a schedule for each and every soul," I thought of her. A year hadn't passed since she had fulfilled her commitment to the earth, leaving her persona and ego behind. I sought to touch her but now, as part of the Universal Soul and Mind, she was beyond those confines.

"Dearest Julia," Hammal restarted his conference, pulling me back to the present, "the development of a soul is much more complex than you might imagine. Each and every life that touches the earth has a schedule. There is an ultimate plan that must include the *currents* of the universe as part of the total consideration. Just transiting the physical body from life to death and from death to life is very traumatic for a soul."

He paused to let me orient myself, then moved on.

"There are groups of angels dedicated to assisting souls enter and exit from the material world," he continued. "These angels function as guides. When it is time for a soul to leave the earth, the guides hover around the individual for a couple of days prior to the scheduled death. They clear the air to make space for the soul's transcendence."

My mind flashed to my mother's last days in the hospital. The night she died, the unlit room was filled with a rosy luminescence—I could feel the presence of helpers all around her.

"Once the body is recognized as dead," Hammal continued, "it will still usually take a total of three days for the soul to leave its body. And as soon as the soul has left, the angels, who have helped the soul transcend, remain to rebalance the energies of the physical beings who were related to the departed."

My thoughts then moved to the night my father died. When I entered the house where he lived with my mother, I felt nothing. His presence, his vibration, was not there. But as my sister and I packed the car with the catered supper for the day of his funeral, I found him. He was at the restaurant he had managed and came home with us in the car.

Three days earlier, he had collapsed and died in a matter of hours. He hadn't realized that he had left his body and was questioning *why* my sister and I had suddenly flown to New Jersey from Miami. I sensed his confusion.

"Julia..." I was startled by Hammal's voice. "...do you think it is easier to be born or to die?"

For me the answer was easy. Dying really didn't seem to be all that difficult. When my time came, I knew that I would just take a deep breath and merge with the light, I said.

I had already touched the light in this life when I went wandering out of my body deliberately looking for it one afternoon. And I had tranquilly found it. The freedom was awesome. So I concluded that being born must be more difficult than dying.

Besides, just the idea of coming onto the earth into a situation where one learns through pain wasn't all that appealing. And having been a very late birth, and a baby that the doctors had to practically pry out of the womb, I figured that I must have known something. Yes, being born had to be a lot more difficult.

"Dying is not as easy as it might seem," Hammal began to explain. However, it *is* easier to die than to be born.

"But in order to be able to leave your body, the work your soul has set out to do in a particular lifetime must be completed," he said emphatically.

"Once your obligations are fulfilled, the currents of the universe, the forces that enable you to continue on your individual lifeline from life to life, must be *positioned* properly and the *right* moment to transcend your body must be awaited," he elaborated. "So it is not really easy to die and leave the physical body. Everything the soul has undertaken to do on earth must be accomplished and the energy for the soul to continue on its particular path must be clear.

"But to leave the peace of the Universal Soul and the spherical forces and transit onto the earth to enter into a body is more traumatic than dying.

"Preparations for that journey are also more complex because the space for that transit has to be created," he continued to explain. "The *energy* on which the soul can come through into a body has to be *found*.

"A birth is not at all a haphazard event although it sometimes may appear to be so. The maneuvering however is very complex. A soul cannot come into a body through the body of another embodied soul (i.e., the physical mother) unless the hierarchy of that soul is right and can line up with the incarnating soul.

"This means that not only generations of souls are considered but *eternities* of souls must be aligned to find the proper lodging for the incarnating soul. It is a tremendous feat of energy engineering.

"The soul must be not only be fitted with the right family but mesh with the necessary vibrations in regard to friends, birthplace, race, sex and so on to best accommodate the karma for each particular lifetime.

"You, Julia, are here for your last life and have requested that those you have ever loved be brought to you."

Hammal paused, expecting questions. But I was too surprised to ask. So he continued.

"Even after a soul has looked everywhere for its proper place and is ready to be born, the situation may still have to be reevaluated," he explained, saying that if a soul that is about to enter a body has an obstacle relative to energy, the incarnation may be a no go.

"Perhaps, re-intuited, rather than reevaluated is more accurate," he clarified. "The situation may have to be *re-*

intuited since souls work on pure energy, not intelligence or emotion.

"Outside of a body, a soul's intuition has nothing to do with thought; thought is not recognized as it exists on the earth. Beyond the physical realm, the soul is considered part of the Universal Mind—the Universal Soul and Universal Mind balance each other, functioning as one.

"The movement of souls beyond the physical is also dramatically different from the traumatic transits a soul encounters as it develops from life to life.

"Outside of the body, all souls function in a light-filled tapestry of energy—a *blanket of threads* in constant flux that works perfectly as a whole. If one thread is missing we all feel it."

The powerful, mental picture recalled my moment in the light.

I questioned, "If everything is so closely guided, why are there lost souls? But then, if a soul is not on its path, how can it be guided?"

Hammal had disclosed that many souls on the earth have no discipline or direction but, just the same, they are allowed freedom of choice. I pictured myself in a strange city without a map.

Things were getting clearer. I thought of the Bible, the moral map, the set of directions meant to illustrate behavior on the earth; it hadn't worked. So now the Cosmic Angelic Force was here; this had never happened before.

I reminded myself that there was a plan. I would be patient until Hammal revealed all that was necessary for it to function.

"And Julia."

"Yes?"

"I want you to know that *chronology is a myth.* Yesterday is still working as today; today is yesterday." Hammal had read my mind again. "Sequence has nothing to do with meaning. But we will talk of this at a later time."

A fleeting thought of Icail, Bringer of Forseen Light, darted through my musings. I heard the angel say "I bring you knowledge to help you with what is to *come*, also its opposite, the knowledge that has *gone*...which for me becomes *forseen* light."

When Hammal departed, I continued to accompany the little girl and her mother for a few more miles on the train to Philadelphia.

I got off in Miami to greet Havah whose weekend had turned into a week and some days.

I could barely contain my excitement. Holding my breath, I slowly lifted the golden Cancer from its blue velvet box.

"It's beautiful. I love it. Thank you," Havah whispered.

Her wide eyes traveled over the shimmering pendant, assessing the fine detail and delicate form that had come from the pool of freely flowing creative energy offered by the Universal Mind.

III
Matters of the Soul

Chapter 10

Functions of the Soul

"Dearest Julia, Your soul is your direction. It is your truth of understanding. It is love so clear that you <u>see</u> because you love." Hammal Cahone

I awakened early. A surprise call from the airport—my lover was on his way home. Joy, joy, joy!

A lightweight blanket covered the bed and the windows were opened wide to the damp chill of a mild Miami winter morning. Just outside, perennially perched in the dew-drenched palm, our mockingbird heralded the good news. I snuggled into the warm pillows, anticipating the sound of his key in the lock. It was wonderful to be alive!

His twenty-minute drive from the airport would seem endless; I reached for my notes to fill the time...

"Dearest Julia, Your soul is your direction. It is your truth of understanding. It is love so clear that you *see* because you love."

I felt every syllable of the lengthy lecture from the night before. My direction was clear. The only thing I wanted from this life was to be with my man and my animals and to help the Angelic Forces. I was very directed in my soul, and felt very loved.

"Souls are huge, powerful and much more complex than you would ever imagine," Hammal continued.

"There are highly evolved souls here to help, right now. I will describe two of them so that you are able to understand what an evolved soul is and the power it has.

"There is an embodied soul that has lived alone in a cave on the earth for centuries. He works with the Cosmic Angelic Force. No one ever sees him yet his cosmic extensions reach far out into the cosmos to bring light, love and truth to the earth. Feeling no pain or hurt, he can extend himself out beyond the boundaries of his physical body. He has saved the earth from many disasters and is one whom I have introduced to you.

"There is also a woman, embodied on the earth, whose soul is extended cosmically as the soul of another earth and who is simultaneously sowing seeds of creation on still another earth.

"As one of the architects of the universe, this soul also belongs to the Cosmic Angelic Force, the United Aquarian Force—a force of change that brings new light into the universe. She is a member of the Marahsundra Force which balances by bouncing light and utilizes the joy of creativity that directs the arts everywhere. She is also one of the Kamzftz Force of builders and directors that build from within and the Ferignunoonme Forces that direct ultimate perspective. The Force balances from without so that what is being built from within does not crumble.

"This soul works directly with two other cosmically extended souls at this time, also embodied on the earthly plane. Both are extensions her soul created centuries ago—souls that continue to evolve *on their own*. She and one of her extensions simultaneously work in the cosmos with hydro-galactic meters, which are cosmic weights. And there is more.

"Working directly with the people of the earth, she has been incarnated as Elizabeth the First, Joan of Arc, Nefertiti, a powerful Egyptian king, a Mayan priestess and others. The woman of whom I speak has created six soul extensions during her current lifetime who are now part of the human race. Just as the human body can propagate itself, souls can create souls, jointly or on their own.

"This means there are six souls that she has recently created. They are incarnated in six different bodies, none of which she will physically meet in this life. However, the six extensions will feed knowledge back to her, their creator, for three years as part of their responsibility. After that they continue on their own.

"One soul has been embodied as a female beggar in India who, when given an offering, shines such loving light into the eyes of her benefactors that it touches their souls. And for your information, the greater the soul creating the extensions, the more evolved the extensions.

"Like you, Julia, the master-soul has many animals; angels surround her. And like you, one of her dogs is the soul extension of one of her earlier soul extensions.

"Are you beginning to see how tremendously powerful an evolved soul can be and how closely joined and interwoven we all are?"

The question really hadn't required an answer but, yes, I did see how complex a soul could be. I had tried to picture myself working in all the capacities Hammal described but it was difficult. I also began to realize how restrictive a body is and how much knowledge I had left on the other side of the door before entering onto the earth—how much we all must leave. I did know that when the man I loved was with me, I felt like a giant. We seemed to validate each other, amplify each other's existence.

I looked back at my notes and read...

"Earlier, I spoke of alpha angels on the earth as those with *cosmic* soul extensions. Although beta angels have no cosmic extensions, they may well have soul extensions on the earth.

One you know has recently created a cat, a lizard and a giraffe. I thought that you might also be interested in knowing that monkeys have *descended* from man," Hammal laughed, turning the familiar theory back into itself. "As I previously stated, the human race has come from *infinite* beings.

"And while I have touched on the subject of angelic souls, I want you to know that *fallen* angels do not exist. If you are an angel, you will always be an angel. You will always have the truth of who you are within your soul. Even if you are an angel who is off your path and your angelic qualities are not in use, you are still responsible for that truth in whatever form you are.

"I know that you will be happy to hear that every soul is on its way to becoming an angel with cosmic extensions, a master who will continue to evolve. All souls are forever in the process of evolution. And *all* souls on earth can become alpha angels," he emphasized.

I read on to the next segment of the conference.

"Very highly evolved souls channel the messages from the highest master in the cosmos in which they have chosen to evolve. The vibrations filter down through the spherical forces by way of the angelic forces to reveal the plan or direction that has been given.

"There is no God per se but rather degrees of mastership that are distinct in the different cosmos, continuing on to the Infinite who is Infinite.

"The great spiritual minds that serve to rule and lead on the earth plane are often master souls of *other* universes. They come here to bring their light and vision to this universe. Their souls, like all souls, form a link between the visible, physical universe and the spirit world."

In my soul, I thanked the masters and the Cosmic Angelic Force that came with the vision, the plan, to get the earth back on track.

"When you see an individual walking down the street, you cannot begin to comprehend the degree of cosmic understanding or evolution that soul might possess," Hammal started a new facet of the lecture.

"Consider the woman beggar in India—the soul extension of the master alpha angel who is here to help humanity—how many will look into her eyes and see the light, or depth, of her vision?

"At this time, I wish to clarify the concept of the body as the reflection of the soul," Hammal continued. "This does not mean that a broken or bent body reflects a broken or distorted soul. It merely means that the body mirrors the role which the soul has undertaken in a particular lifetime.

"Look into the eyes to know the soul. Again, this does not mean that one who is without physical sight is without a soul— there are other eyes with which to see.

"The reverse is also true. One who is rich and beautiful by earth standards may not have a compassionate heart or a great soul. A lesson may be unfolding that you would never consider. For instance, given everything but the one thing she really desires, a woman may yearn only to conceive and deliver a healthy baby and, time after time, miscarries; or a materially successful, virile appearing man may find out that he is sterile.

"These are very simple examples so you will better understand that what seems real is in no way a measure of the truth.

Hammal paused again to allow this to settle, then continued to illuminate still another facet. I turned the page.

"And there is more to know of souls," Hammal continued. "One person does not always equal one soul. Sometimes an enormous job must be undertaken or there are several souls who need to learn a particular lesson. So a group will choose to incarnate together in one body.

"One such group soul incarnated as a Russian monk—a very powerful holy man who, through his manipulations, controlled the imperial throne. His karma was to bring a new religion onto the earth but through confused knowledge, things got out of hand. The truth of the group soul was not heeded, and those who were incarnated as Rasputin are still paying enormous karma for the damage done."

Hammal paused once more to allow me to think this over, then went on to say, "Occasionally one powerful soul will split into several different bodies. This is not the same as a soul extension. This is an actual split—one soul that will rejoin itself after the work is completed. Historically, various European monarchs, in order to avoid wars and facilitate diplomacy, were actually one soul that incarnated into several bodies. This is also one of the reasons why many of the rulers had a great fondness for each other.

"Besides split souls and group souls, there can be soul fragments. When a soul once touches the earth, it cannot leave until its work here is done. If a soul must go or chooses to go to another domain for a time, a fragment is left on the earth. This can be in the form of a lizard, or whatever, that will remain on the earth while the major part of the soul takes its leave. There are other kinds of soul fragments which we will discuss later.

"Trees and flowers can have souls; these are not the same as souls that incarnate in human form. Even a rock can have a soul. It may not have the nervous system with which to sense physical pain, but if it has a soul, it can suffer pangs of compassion. What I have told you may shed some additional light on why all things created must be respected."

Hammal paused again to await another segment of the message. At the time, I thought this was a great deal of information for one conference but reminded myself that the channels were open. Planetary movements sometimes interfered. There were stagnant days, and nights when the airwaves crackled with static. One night Hammal and several angels had to clear my throat chakra of the static I had picked up while out of my body. For this conference, Hammal had taken optimum advantage of the clear air.

He continued. "There are souls that may inhabit a body just long enough to complete their karma, and then another soul may take over the same body..."

This was something I had not considered.

"...like your student, Jesse, who survived a serious illness at the age of seven but can't remember a thing about her life before that time. This is because life for her did not exist before the age of seven. She is not the original incarnating soul."

That's a show stopper, I thought.

"The original soul needed only the first seven years to work out its karma and departed. It was all part of the plan *before* the souls entered onto the earth.

"There was also a soul exchange for the mother of the young man you know as Ivan."

I recalled a very giving and gentle woman before she fell into a coma. When she finally emerged, her personality had changed radically. The family was shocked at the transition. Unable to let go of the mother they loved, the *body* remained with the family while her *soul* continued on as scheduled.

"Another soul entered her body quite legally in a last minute change in plans. The energy and timing had been right for the second incarnating soul to take over the body and work out its karma," Hammal explained.

"Souls can also temporarily visit the earth to coexist with an embodied soul by agreement in order to commit an act of heroism, deliver an important message, or the like.

"There is still much more to know about souls. But first and foremost, you must remember that the function of the soul is *truth*. When a soul, through careless or confused knowledge, becomes separated from the truth of its being, it grieves. And when one soul suffers, we all do.

"To stay in touch with the truth, a soul *must* pray. This means that you must live in a state of connection with the angelic forces. In this way you become part of the universal energy flow, where light, protection and healing come *to* you and flow *through* you. Prayer is your link between the physical and the spiritual. We will talk more of this soon."

With that, the lecture had ended. I closed my notebook.

The timing was perfect. The key turned in the lock and the front door opened.

I quickly slipped my notes back onto the night stand, slid down beneath the covers and sucked in my breath in anticipation...

Chapter 11

The Spirit,
Cadaverous Spirits

"Dearest Julia, Your spirit is directed energy. It functions as an indivisible combination of will, intention and vision—but it's force can be broken."

Hammal Cahone

I felt hollow.

Thanksgiving Day always held a weight for me.

This may sound like a contradiction, but many holidays have an empty, oppressive atmosphere. Great festivities are planned and anticipations are unfulfilled; loved ones are all too often painfully absent. Familiar souls, having left their bodies, hover in close, adding more weight—especially those that seemed to have been lost in life.

I was putting the last of five dozen white roses in an arrangement when Hammal arrived.

"I wish you a joyous holiday," He greeted me.

"Thank you," I replied.

I was delighted that Hammal had come. He always brought me great peace and his presence added energy to the day. Even when his lectures weren't the most joyous, they were timely. And today was perfect for a lecture on the spirit.

"Your spirit is directed energy," Hammal began. "It functions as an *indivisible* combination of will, intention and vision—but it's *force* can be broken."

Having made his introduction, he went on to explain that everyone has a soul and a spirit.

"Your soul is your soul. It is the truth of your being; it is who you are and is *never* selected," he said.

"But your spirit is determined according to the *needs* of your soul and the work you have agreed to accomplish in each incarnation. So the strength or force of your spirit can *change* from one life to the next.

"As an example, if a particular soul has chosen to unify all knowledge of this universe (admittedly, an ambitious karma to fulfill), that soul must be given a spirit of great strength," Hammal illustrated. "It is in this way that the individual soul receives the spirit it needs—you are given what is necessary, according to the work you have agreed to accomplish.

"So your will, intentions and vision combine indivisibly as your spirit," Hammal recapped. "Your spirit is not your *ultimate* direction; your ultimate direction is your soul. Your soul is truth and always the same.

"Functioning together, the spirit and soul work out problems. The process begins with your spirit and is completed with your soul—you *feel* through your spirit and *know* in your soul. Your spirit tests and your soul remembers. Much like karma, it is the nature of the human race to weigh and measure. This is necessary in order to learn.

"Your will *usually* travels with your soul since your chosen spirit *generally* works continuously with the direction your soul tries to achieve. I say 'usually' and 'generally' because an individual spirit can be broken or lost. It is more of a *living* thing than people realize.

"When your spirit is lost, you will have no *strength* of will. You can have all the power in the world, but if you are unable to face your will, which is your desire (your direction on earth) you have nothing.

"Even so, your soul can still be beautiful and remains with you—and your soul is, indeed, more important than your spirit. But should you lose your spirit, it is because of weakness.

"Sometimes a spirit is broken on this earth for the sake of individual learning as part of a lesson and karma. But some spirits are never broken.

"Your spirit, Julia, was never meant to be broken. Your grandmother tried, but couldn't do it. Havah's spirit couldn't be broken. But most parents will break their children's spirits. However, some children are too strong and the few spirits that are not broken are not supposed to be."

"One of the unresolved parent-child issues that over-shadow holiday festivities," I thought, picturing holiday tables as Woody Allen satires and thinking that the whole mess was sad—grieving souls, broken spirits. No wonder the holidays get everyone down.

Hammal quickly balanced my analogy with cosmic perspective. "The group soul that was Rasputin had a powerful spirit," he noted. "But the souls who were Rasputin will not be allowed a powerful spirit again for a long time due to the damage they did. Until those individuals can appreciate and use their power for the good of the universe, their spirits will be easily broken. Power is earned. It is withheld when abused.

"This is not to say that all those whose wills have been broken have abused power in the past. Some have, but others have come here to learn how to be comfortable with them-selves, to release guilt, to learn of love—these are examples. So a strong spirit is not always needed for the debt that is under-taken."

That certainly added another dimension. The more infor-mation Hammal brought to light from the cosmos, the more I realized how little I understood from my nearsighted, earthly point of view.

"Spirits that *are* broken," he continued, "are broken to certain degrees. This does not mean that the individual whose spirit has been broken becomes immediately weak, but it does mean that vast *insecurities* will stop that person's intentions.

"After losing your spirit, you can regain a direction and possibly some spirit, but usually not in the original degree. Once your spirit is broken, your decision-making will be wishy-washy, and your ability to sense vibrations won't be as clear.

"In many books, especially those in Indian philosophy, you are told that you will 'know the truth' or 'sense the vibration' of truth. This, however, is hampered if your spirit isn't as attuned as it should be.

"Mothers are generally the parents who break the force (the will) of their child's spirit, but this is not the actual spirit itself.

"Broken wills result in cadaverous spirits—*energy* (force) *without the direction of vision*. These cadaverous spirits hang in the sky, without movement.

"I wish to clarify," Hammal explained, "that although responsible for breaking the spirit, a mother will not accrue negative karma for this because it is in the nature of a mother's insecurities to do this."

He continued. "At this time, when many people on earth are giving up their souls, 85% of the people on earth do not have their spirits intact." Hammal's statistic was impressive.

My god, I thought, if you must feel in your spirit (which is broken) in order to *know* in your soul (which is your direction that *isn't* directed*)* plus have free will, it was no wonder people were confused and giving up their souls.

I considered that only about 15% of the people on the earth have the full force of the spirits they were born with intact.

These, I assumed, would be the leaders on the earth—the shepherds of the flock. They would have immense responsibilities and suffer tremendous karma if they misdirected their energies or led others astray.

Again I turned to thoughts of the Universal Mind and how Hammal said that the accelerated energies coming into this solar system's reign of thought were being misinterpreted. I recalled the duelling energies of Light and Dark.

More thought fragments floated in the vapid, hollow holiday air. I was desperate for something concrete on which to build hope.

Hammal offered it. "If a soul can touch upon great truth," he said, "it will become spirit, a directed energy of great intention. A spirit so developed can be a driving force which, with good intention, will affect other souls."

The great truths the angels are bringing could ignite souls and direct them to seek more light, I thought with optimism.

"Please tell me about cadaverous spirits."

Hammal replied, "As I have stated, cadaverous spirits result when people give up their wills. More precisely, cadaverous spirits are the residue of the *force* of human will—dead spirits that remain trapped on the earth until the living physical bodies of the people the spirits belong to die.

"You must understand that a will is a living thing," Hammal repeated. "A lost will, or spirit, becomes a cadaverous spirit. Groups of cadaverous spirits clutter the air and block the rays. These dead spirits rest over water, unable to go anywhere.

"They are almost equal to human weight. Just as different people have different weights, stronger spirits have heavier weights. But, as I have stated, the stronger spirits are generally not broken.

"Are the cadaverous spirits a problem for the incoming light, like the grieving souls?" I inquired.

"Because the broken wills are still related to the people who own them, the placement of cadaverous spirits can be a problem if too many group together and block the light. When they are distributed evenly, only a thin layer is formed; this can be easily penetrated.

"So in answer to your question, cadaverous spirits can be a problem, but no where near the extent of the grieving souls.

"It also might interest you to know that the percentage of cadaverous spirits is high in the Devil's Triangle because there is a vortex that holds them there."

I tried to put together the information Hammal had given. He said my spirit is *energy* that travels with my soul. More specifically, my spirit is directed energy, an indivisible unit of will-intention-vision.

This means that if the *force* of my will is weakened, the clarity of my vision and strength of my intentions is lessened.

Once my will is crushed, I can no longer make clear-cut, quick decisions. Nor can I recognize truth as readily as I did as a child. My vision, my decision making, my ability to see truth is diminished, according to the amount of force I have lost.

If my spirit is intact with its original force, it is for a purpose. If it is damaged or diminished in its primary might, it is the result of a lesson, karma, or a lack of strength on my part.

Once my will has been fractured, the residue of its force joins other dead spirits. It becomes a cadaverous spirit to just hang in the sky with other broken wills, remaining there until I die.

Before Hammal brought the conference to an end, he emphasized that the spirit, although it is a help to the soul, does not determine the ultimate direction of the soul. "The soul is still beautiful and can still be with you even if your spirit is broken," he said. "Your ultimate direction, your individual truth, and the direction of your soul never changes."

Hammal then relayed some personal information that would benefit family members and some of the people who would attend Thanksgiving dinner. He again wished me a happy holiday and departed.

It was time to meet Havah, Leah, my sister, her husband and my nephew Steven. We were all going to Mom's house for the festivities.

For Mom, holidays were always ceremoniously observed and included cut crystal and silver on a perfectly set table laden with more food than it was meant to hold. There was still more food on the buffet, and endless trips to the kitchen to bring out new dishes.

I could almost smell her stuffed cabbage, crisp-skinned, tender turkey, candied sweet potatoes, spinach au gratin, and garlicky cucumbers in sour cream, and hear "Where's the cranberry sauce?" before we began the short ride to her house. Gil, Carmen and other friends would be joining us, bringing wines, nuts and other goodies.

Overwhelmed and delighted by the huge white basket, overflowing with five dozen white roses that barely fit into the wide-open trunk of my car, Mom gasped as I wrestled the arrangement through the front door and carefully set it on her glass coffee table.

Havah brought a Sacher Torte and a plate of colorful petit fours. Leah carried her special homemade bread. My sister offered a box of chocolates and a pumpkin pie. Five-year-old Steven proudly held up a card he had made all by himself, and I can't remember all the rest.

Good friends, good food, good family, good spirits—the day was looking up...

Chapter 12

Questions, Misconceptions, A Riddle Solved.

What is God? The Bible? Heaven? Hell? Sin?
What am I personally here to do?

Many of my questions were being answered, so I was
excited when Hammal made an early morning call. Little did I
know that I was in for one of the heaviest sessions I would ever
have. What is it they say—be careful what you ask for? And be
careful when you ask for more.

"Dearest Julia," Hammal began, "I know you have many
questions and from our many undertakings together throughout
the cosmos, I know of your impatient nature. But you have
learned much already.

"You have learned of the simple structure of the universe.

"You have learned that you are an infinite being, completely derived from infinite beings.

"You now know that your body is dense energy that
reflects of your soul.

"You realize that you are part of the spherical force, which
is a combination of soul energy and angelic force.

"You comprehend that creative thought drives the spherical forces, creating greater and lesser energy, ever-expanding in
an infinite creation.

"You are aware that your energy is linked to every other energy in the universe, and that you can travel throughout the cosmos on currents of energy.

"You now appreciate the scope in which you, consciously and unconsciously, are affected by every other soul's energy and vibrations.

"You have recognized that you are a receptor for knowledge and can receive as much light and as many gifts from the Universal Mind as your mind will allow.

"You have gained an understanding of how a soul functions and the way spirit works in conjunction with soul.

"But these are things that you knew as part of the Universal Soul and the Cosmic Angelic Force. We are just reopening the doors to channels that you are already familiar with.

"When one reincarnates, no more or less is given to fulfill your karma. These gifts, as you now know, also include your spirit and your will.

"When move along your karmic path, more gifts are given so that you can continue on. In order for you to fulfill your karma, it is time to unseal the doors that we have begun to access.

"The work that you sense you must do is already being done through your cosmic extensions. We will tell you what more is necessary. Until then please be patient.

"For the time being, I can tell you that the concepts of heaven, hell, god, and sin, as they are known to humanity, are strictly earthly concepts. They are part the framework humanity uses for direction. And as you well know, the Bible, the book of direction, has been misinterpreted by the human race.

"I am aware that the concept of sin has bothered you for some time, Julia, and I can tell you that in the light of truth, there is *no* sin. There is only the progression toward knowledge that ultimately results in positive growth of the soul.

"Sins are but limited explanations of the hardships that humanity imposes on *itself.* They are blinders that shield the human race from truth.

"The motions, vibrations, or actions initiated through ill intent that I have spoken of are human weaknesses, not sins. And so-called transgressions, undertaken with good intent, are not even weaknesses. They are merely steps on a journey to self-discovery.

"The mythological road to hell is not paved with good intentions. But if hell and the road to it existed, good intentions would have no place on it. Being pure in heart is what matters.

"I repeat, there is only a progression toward knowledge that ultimately results in the positive growth of the soul.

"Various earthly concepts have encompassed the idea of good and evil. Ancient Greece gave birth to the idea of moral harm, regarding evil as a necessary defect in *human* nature. The ancient Egyptians counted eight blindfolds that referred to the eyes and an inability to *see.*

"Buddhism cites eight motions of the soul, known as the eightfold path, consisting of right intention, right speech, right action, right livelihood, right effort, right-mindedness and right contemplation. These belong to the three major categories: morality, wisdom and *samadhi* (concentration) that form the cornerstones of Buddhism.

"Buddhist dogma, however, holds desire as the root of all evil, believing that once you are without desire you progress spiritually. This notion contains some truth since once you have satisfied all of your desires and debts on the earth, you are free to move on. But desires are sometimes the root of all good because in working out your desires you move past them. When you suppress your desires, you cause yourself more problems.

"The idea of *deadly,* mortal sin emerged full blown in the Catholic Church. First introduced by St. Augustine, seven stages in the downward course of the soul were cataloged by Pope Gregory I in the *Catalogia Saligia* (saligia meaning spirits of weakness).

"Listed first and foremost is the deadly sin of self-pride— the concept being that self before God *leads* to selfishness and then to all other deadly sins, including avarice, lust, envy, gluttony, anger and finally sloth which is the ungrateful distaste for life: apathy, irritation, and low body tone—resulting from unconsciously eating into the heart and one's own negativity.

"The seven deadly sins delineated the tests of life in general. Considered barriers that blocked union with God, perpetrators, deprived of the so-called true end, were said to suffer *death* of the soul.

"Now I tell you that your soul *never* dies. Your soul is your direction and your truth.

"This concept of deadly sin involves much convoluted thought, for the so-called deadliest sin, self-pride, can be the highest *virtue*—self-respect, self-worth, self-compassion, self-forgiveness, self-love—which ultimately leads to love for all.

"Concepts of polarity, good and evil, perfection and imperfection exist only on the earth. Cosmically, there are no such opposites—only greater and lesser good. Each soul is ultimately good and on the way to that understanding.

"I hope this sheds sufficient light on the earthly misconception of sin for you, Julia." Hammal paused.

I nodded, reflecting that sin did not exist, only a human inability to see that caused confused concepts. In fulfilling our desires, our blindfolds are removed, ultimately offering self-knowledge and *positive* growth of our soul, our truth, our direction. In this light, I mused, humanity would have to rethink itself.

"Hell does not exist, either," Hammal continued. "The notion originated because some individuals wanted hell, instead of debt, to rule the earth.

"Since the people of the earth are all so closely associated, the vibrations extended from the individuals who misinterpreted to the rest. So more trauma and confusion was introduced into the collective vibration of humanity.

"I will elaborate if you have a question," Hammal said.

Everything seemed quite understandable. Instead of a clear-cut concept of paying and owing, which was the original plan of the earth, humanity itself turned this simple plan into a very elaborate, torturous, pay-or-else debtor's prison—Hades. I turned the page and signaled, "Please go on."

"Heaven does not exist as a place," Hammal continued. "It is a state of rest in which you are allowed the freedom not to pursue. When you have accomplished something, you are in heaven for a while—in a period of rest that exists on an individual basis only.

"When your work on earth is finished, you continue on. Eventually you will need no form. You will become a flow of energy that nurtures everything—a state in which you need no vehicle to exist, only the teachings of your own soul.

"Although the basic assumption of heaven is incorrect," he said, "there is a capacity in your soul to touch all and to illuminate all roads with your light—this is the greatest peace."

Hammal paused again.

This too seemed quite clear—the earth was a visible, physical world that attempted to project a paradise called heaven—a reflection of the earth, lighter in form and substance but a physical place just the same. This was simply a misconception.

"The concept of god is also a confused notion. When I speak of god, I do not refer to the Universal Soul, or the Universal Mind, or the Infinite that is Infinite. What I speak of is the god of the earth as introduced in the Bible.

"It is true that a god rules this creation. It is also a fact that there is only one true god and that god is the giver and taker of life. God is also love. But the god of the earth is *debt*."

Hammal stopped to be sure I had heard him correctly.

"Debt is the god of the earth," he said and paused again.

"The earth was created because souls needed a place to work off debt," Hammal explained. "So debt truly *rules* this creation—your god is simply debt."

Hammal paused once more to allow me to think this over.

The concept took me by surprise.

I had long released the idea of an anthropomorphic god, a benevolent father, or an omni-protecting father-mother god. I believed in something like the Universal Soul or the outpouring of the One.

This notion of god as debt is going to take a little getting used, I thought, until I realized that Hammal was not redefining the outpouring of the One or challenging the Universal Soul; he was simply correcting our concept of "god" as delineated in the Holy Scriptures—our book of rules. Humanity had mistakenly personified a concept and misinterpreted the meaning.

"It is true that the god described in the Bible is truly the *only* god that exists on the earth." But the Bible is describing debt," Hammal continued.

"When you come here, you *must* obey the laws of the earth, the Law of Debt. This is your god.

"Debt gives you life-—life is "breathed" into you so you can work out your karma on earth.

"Debt also takes your life—when you are finished with the work you set out to do and have fulfilled your karma, you can leave the earth and ultimately your cycle of incarnations, no longer needing life on earth.

"And...the ultimate lesson of debt is love. In this way your god, your debt, is *love*."

Hammal waited for me to ask questions. It all made sense.

Something was milling in the back my brain, but I couldn't quite put it together. I thought back to the first night Hammal appeared.

I could hear him say, "At this time, the earth is returning to the knowledge it has lost for seven circles and is again advancing to the seventh circle to gain new knowledge.

"Mankind has misunderstood the meaning of the circles. Nothing on earth ever gets to eight. God is earth—God is debt. Debt is dead at eight. Infinity is nine.

"Eight is the highest hope—when you have learned and you know. That is why eight is heaven on earth, when god, or debt, is eliminated. Once you get to eight, souls will be so finely attuned that the earth as it now exists will not be needed. It will transform and another will take its place.

"Eight is freedom from debt, or peace on earth."

I carefully went back over the whole message again, sentence by sentence...

At this time, the earth is returning to the knowledge it has lost for seven circles and is again advancing to the seventh circle to gain new knowledge.

This is where we are now—at the final level of our present circle. We are edging up to the point of transition at which the human race must acquire the new knowledge that it has been lacking.

Mankind has misunderstood the meaning of the circles. Nothing on earth ever gets to eight.

Earlier I had discovered the notion of eight was similar to the musical octave where eight is actually the first number of the next round. If you recall...

Do-re-me-fa-sol-la-ti-do is the musical scale. *Do* is one, *re* is two, *me* is three, *fa* is four, *sol* is five, *la* is six, *ti* is seven, and *do* finishes the octave. But *"do"* is not really eight when you are to <u>continue</u> on. It is, rather, the first note of the next octave—or the first level of the next circle or round.

God is earth—god is debt.

Hammal had just explained that the earth was created in order to work off debt. So god was the earth and also debt.

113

Debt is dead at eight.
Eight equals one. In the first level of the next circle, debt will no longer exist.

Infinity is nine.
Infinity exists beyond the earth's circles of incarnation.

Eight is the highest hope—when you have learned and you know. That is why eight is heaven on earth, when God, or debt, is eliminated. Once you get to eight, souls will be so finely attuned that the earth as it now exists will not be needed. It will transform and another will take its place. Eight is freedom from debt or peace on earth.
Heaven is a resting place, when you are free not to pursue. The earth, at eight, will become a place where humanity will no longer need to pay and owe.

I now understood.
The circles went from one to seven; eight was the pivotal point between levels. Eight was the first level of the next circle or round and meant freedom from debt. Eight was the resting place. It was heaven on earth, mission accomplished.

When the earth reached eight, it would be no longer be a physical earth. It would have become free to move to the next level in its own evolution where it would need no form and become part of the flow of energy that nurtured everything—touching all, illuminating all with light.

Once the earth transformed to eight, another soul, another planet would take the place of the earth.

There would always be an earth for the souls that needed to learn the lessons taught by the earth, but not the earth of this universe that is etched by the injuries of seven former destructions and eight incarnations.

Humanity as a whole would have taken a step forward, allowing the earth to evolve as well.

Beyond the evolution of the earth, from level to level and circle to circle, is Infinity. Infinity is nine.

One of my biggest questions was answered.

"This is very much to absorb, Julia. Would you like to stop at this time?" Hammal asked.

"No, no, not at all. Please go on." I was heady with the new knowledge and totally out of my body. I didn't realize how exhausted I was. I just wanted to know more.

"Just the same," Hammal insisted, "we will take a break and allow the vibration to settle. We will meet again tonight after the sun has set."

It still was morning. I busied myself around the house, bleaching the white tile floors—something I did when I needed to ground myself, balance my reeling brain, and establish a distance from the incoming information.

It was mechanical therapy. I set my mind on automatic and worked mindlessly touching the ground on my hands and knees. For hours, I monotonously dipped my sponge into the pail of bleach, detergent and water, soaked a small section of the floor, let the mixture do its work, scrubbed the stubborn spots in the grout, blotted up the grey-tinged residue, wiped with a dry towel, and repeated the rhythmic sequence again and again. The windows were wide open to a bright, breezeless day and the powerful attic fan sucked out the piercing scent of chlorine.

Later that afternoon, I surveyed the job. The floors where white, white, white, my body was as exhausted as my mind, and the house sparkled. I fell dead asleep for hours.

When I awoke, my head was heavy with questions.

Would the earth just physically vanish from this solar system or would another earth take its place immediately?

When the earth reached eight, would the solar system, and this entire universe also move on?

Would humanity just disappear or dissolve into light?

Did the meek inherit another earth? I later learned the meek were those who would not evolve but would be destroyed with the earth to become grieving souls for a long time.

But my questions wouldn't be answered this night. Hammal had other information to deliver and started to unfold his revelations the moment he arrived.

My head felt like lead; I really wanted to just rest and float off on a cloud. But I had insisted on the meeting, against Hammal's concerns for me. So I took a deep breath and started to write.

"The Bible it is a book of *direction*," Hammal began. It is a book of vision that was brought into being with the third earth to help guide humanity. A history of former earths, it speaks of the future of the world and the destiny of each soul, according to the journey the soul chooses for itself.

He paused.

"The Bible has come into being six times. Every time the earth fragments and is reconstructed, it will have the Bible. The books of the Bible and events in the Bible will reoccur in the same order. What we are talking about here is *direction*.

"However, with each reconstruction the pieces of both the earth and the Bible do not go together in their *original* direction. This is why there are faults in the earth and why the Bible is confusing. Each time the story is told, it is told with minor changes.

"Biblical concepts are for the most part misunderstood just as man's everyday existence is misunderstood. We all live in daily circumstances that offer us the options described in the Bible. Each of us is *a living bible;* we are not books to memorize but living replicas of the characters described in the Bible. This includes their directions and often their confusions.

As a book of direction, the Bible shows the weaknesses and failings of humanity. It illustrates how individuals can lose their direction. It also gives guidance on how to maintain your direction.

"Moses, for instance, was egotistical and became confused, fearful and lost—clearly a character study. Cain and Abel, too, illustrate direction. But I will talk more of this at a later time.

"Much insight can be gained by recognizing the Bible as a history of former earths and as a vision of the earth's destiny. Understanding of humanity is acquired by studying the direction and paths of Biblical characters."

At this point, Hammal broke off his conference.

"You are much more tired than you know, Julia. The energy you have expended in receiving this new information has drained you. We really must stop for now."

Hammal was right and this time I knew it.

It took several days for me to regain most of my energy. Admittedly, my impatience and hunger for knowledge had gotten the better of me. But undaunted as usual, I pushed on to test the god-debt idea in the Bible.

I went to the beginning, Genesis 1:1, and everywhere I saw the word God, I changed it to debt.

In the beginning God created the heavens and the earth.

I translated, "In the beginning the heavens and the earth were created by debt."

According to Hammal, the earth was brought into existence to work out debt, paying and owing, in order to learn compassion, love, respect and appreciation. It worked. I skipped to Genesis 1:26.

And God said, Let us make Mankind in our image, after our likeness...So God created Mankind in his own image, in the image of God he created him; male and female he created them...

I had some difficulty with this, so when Hammal dropped in to check on my recuperation, I asked for help.

Hammal explained that this meant that the law of karma or debt was placed into the human race.

"Moreover," he said, "man is not god since debt does not make up humanity's total existence. Soul is different from debt. We may owe god-debt but are *directed* in the payment by our souls."

I continued to read...

...and let them (mankind) have dominion over the fish of the sea, and over the birds of the air, and over the cattle, and over all the earth, and over every creeping thing that creeps on the earth.

"This means that humanity has *free choice* over every-thing in the earthly arena—the animals, birds and even the care of the earth," Hammal said. "Dominion refers to the *responsibility* of free choice.

"The Bible is not saying that the *soul* of an incarnating human is greater than the soul of an animal, only that a greater responsibility is carried."

A highly evolved animal may have a greater heart, more compassion and be a cosmically extended soul, like my cat Baba who, after many lives as a human, had finished on the earth plane and reincarnated as a cat to be one of my teachers in this life. But humanity *owes* more. Our unconscious truth, the direction of our soul, knows what our journey here is all about. This means our debt to *all* life is greater.

...and God (Debt) said...Be fruitful and multiply, replenish the earth, and subdue it...

Hammal helped here as well. "We are here to be creative," he said, "to use the transmissions of the Universal Mind fruit-fully.

"We are here to evolve in our souls, to enhance the spheri-cal forces, to reflect universal truths and multiply the light of universal knowledge."

Replenish the earth, I thought, seemed clear enough. Now if only we actually did it, the earth wouldn't be where it is today.

"To subdue the earth," Hammal explained, "means to overcome your debts, to fulfill your karma. Once you've gone past all that you desire of the earth and have learned of self-love, compassion, and respect and can forgive yourself and others, you have subdued or gone past the lessons of the earth and you can continue on. But if you are an individual who does not respect your karma, then you are not respecting the nature of your soul, the nature of truth, or the nature of god."

I began again to contemplate debt as god, and the earth as god, thinking that if we have dominion over the earth, this means that we ultimately have dominion over god.

Think about it.

If god is debt and god is the earth, once we have fulfilled our karma and need only to listen to the direction of our soul, it all fits together.

This means that we will have learned love, appreciation and compassion. We will have evolved beyond our need for everything the earth has to offer. At this time, we will be free of our indebtedness to the physical earth, the physical earth itself, and also to the god of the earth.

I thought back to the chant of the 1970s, "God is dead"... or was it God is debt?

I thanked Hammal for his unscheduled visit and his help.

I was still weak from the days before. Touching the information again, made my head spin. I was out of my body—it was time to ground myself once more.

The floors still looked good. Thank goodness, the garden needed weeding.

The warm sunlight gave me sustenance. As I slowly knelt to pull the tiny weeds my body began to feel more substantial. I paced myself carefully, worked for a short while, thanked the sun for his help, and went back to bed.

There are some things, like controlling my enthusiasm, I guess I'll just never learn.

Chapter 13
What is Karma? Why Pain?

"Dearest Julia, Your actions are your works; your soul is your truth—you build your own karmic path."
Hammal Cahone

I love to make jewelry; it is the legacy of my excursions into other worlds where I seek out treasure and bring it back to the earth. Today, a bird whose body became a snake that wound around an open lattice work was emerging as a powerful design beneath my fingers.

My new gift from the universe, the 6-inch cuff would be one of the most thrilling pieces I had ever undertaken, along with a gold and turquoise chameleon collar and an immense silver scarab whose wings were seared by flames.

When cast, the bracelet would weigh half-a-pound of shimmering 18-karat gold. But my thoughts hadn't yet embraced this sobering reality. I just flew free on the currents to magical places, creating and knowing that whatever I needed would come, and somehow it always did.

As I sculpted, bits and pieces of a poem I had written pecked at my mind, something to do with treasure and a path. I strained unsuccessfully to recite it.

The longer I worked, the more I needed to know exactly what it was I had written. Finally the need to know overcame my excitement with the piece; I started to tear through the old notebooks in which I had secreted my most cherished early writings.

The poem surfaced in a stack yellowed papers. Elated, I carefully unfolded the brittle page to find that the words of a seventeen-year-old still held great meaning for me.

Beside a road, I saw a rugged path.
And just by chance, or maybe fate it was,
I journeyed on the path until it lead
Into a forest deep where life was not.
But still I journeyed on for many hours.
Uphill, I climbed, not always keeping fast
My course, for many sideways lured me from my path.

Sometimes I traveled quickly, sometimes not,
Until I reached a mountain top
Where back upon the road, through mists, I glanced
Just as I had so many times before.

Now on this mountain top, I found a pool
That was as clear and quiet as was deep.
And looking down into its depth, I fathomed not
For in the depths and darkness hidden were
Its many treasures known but to the earth
And to the tree whose shade upon it fell.
I knew that here was where I must remain.
So I may, too, the pool with treasures fill.

Yes, that's what I was looking for. That's exactly how I saw myself when I worked: on a private mountain top diving, safe and sheltered, into a deep, dark, crystalline pool filled with treasure. I had no other no thought but to add to the treasure. Satisfied, I went back to work.

The soft, pliable bracelet continued to unfold under my surgical scalpel. Carving and heating bits of green wax over an alcohol lamp, I dripped the liquid wax, drop by drop, onto the work in progress, recarved the form, again and again addressed the details, continually refining the design—a slow, meticulous process.

It was early afternoon and I sat hunched over my work-bench in the moss-blackened coral rock studio set deep in the subtropical growth where only those who hunted for the gravel roofed, ancient hideaway could find it. Only occasionally someone would stumble onto the private winding road that wandered past the small secluded house.

Nikki, my miniature poodle, was curled up on the ruby red oriental rug. Before he died, at the age of 23, I had asked him to come back to be with me as a royal standard; a year later, he did. Counting both lives, he has been with me for a total of 34 years. Even now, as I write, the same loving vibration is em-bodied in the 80 exquisite pounds stretched out at my feet.

As I worked on the bracelet, words and phrases from the poem echoed in the air...rugged path...the lures of sideways...a forest deep where life was not.

I had been describing my own karmic path and its rest stops where sometimes I traveled quickly, sometimes not.

When I did reach a plateau in the work—heaven, as Hammal called it—there would be a crest where I could look back over the terrain I had covered. I had done this many times before. But like all memories, mists tended to cloud the view.

Then there was a particular mountain top where I could travel while still in my body—a place where I knew I needed to be. Here I could fly on the currents and bring back treasure to fill the pool.

I began to think that we have been so indoctrinated in the negatives of debt and karma, of paying and owing, that as soon as we hear the word karma or debt, we become uneasy.

But if no sin exists in the greater scheme of things (only steps on the road to self-discovery) and everyone is equal in the sight of debt, then each life that we undertake *is* simply another leg of a journey that brings us closer to the truth of our being.

With perfect timing, Hammal appeared. Ready to expand my thoughts, he announced a conference.

I put down my scalpel, extinguished the burner, set my wax in a safe place and picked up a nearby sketch pad to record the incoming message.

"Dearest Julia, the spirit of the earth is to give and we are here to give. Giving and receiving are one and the same.

"The earth is abundant with gifts. The more you can recognize, the more you can accept. The secret is to know how much you need and to recognize the open doors through which you can walk to claim your gifts.

"We are an integral part of this earth, and we must learn to connect with it in order to accept its gifts.

"The physical universe has its own energies which include us. Rather than trying to disassociate ourselves from our physicality, we must allow the energy to flow from us and to us."

He paused and I thought over the concept.

"Then karma and debt are gifts?" I questioned.

"Yes, Julia, but there is more. Karma is something inherent in this universe; debt is a kink in the soul that we each are trying to work out. It is the road to knowledge that has to do with the beginning that is without beginning.

"As soon as anyone touches the earth, karma is incurred; 78% of everything that one does on this earth is karma. Karma however is not always a debt; 22% is chance and accident. But it is something that you agree to undertake and complete, so in that way the 22% is also a debt."

I asked what an "accident" would be.

"For instance, you may be working out your agreed karma when a vibration from a former life surfaces, and you decide to take it on in conjunction with what you are doing at the present. But there are really no accidents," he explained.

"One can achieve more or less than what one has planned in a lifetime," he elaborated. "More is rare.

"And you can work on a few new areas. But when you give, you are given ten times the amount in light—light around you, light from within you, light from your eyes. You are able to reach farther into the depth of your soul.

"If you come to the earth and are too pure, you have to learn of impure vibrations, so that you can understand them," he continued. "That is to say, you have to learn to live among impurity and not become a part of it."

"I had never considered karma in that aspect," I commented.

"You gain karma according to your knowledge. So ignorance of the law is an excuse. But if you have the opportunity to learn the rules and you do not, there is no excuse.

"No one ever completes karma," Hammal went on. "There is always karma, but there is a freedom of mind, a self-forgiveness whereby you free yourself."

"So, I can leave the earth at any time by forgiving myself of my debt?" I asked.

"Yes," Hammal answered.

Something to think about, I mused, reflecting on Hammal's earlier explanation of debt and the original plan for the earth. "Since debt is universal," he explained, "the decision was made to give all souls a chance on the earth, many of whom do not have direction. Add freedom of choice to lack of direction and, in most souls, utter confusion is created. The problem of undirectedness," he lamented, "is the worst. Often, people cannot be directed until they pay their debts in their hearts..."

So self-forgiveness may not be all that easy for an unevolved soul, I reasoned. You must be at certain level to comprehend what you are forgiving before you can forgive it. And if you are evolved to the point of committing your light to the earth, then you are not apt to release yourself or renege on your agreement.

"Regarding karmic debt," Hammal illuminated another aspect, "it is important that we appreciate all organisms as equals. It makes no difference—animal, vegetable, or stone. Without respect and appreciation for all, we *incur* debts to *ourselves.*

"A debt will travel around in our spherical forces up into our high planes, or auras, out of our earthly field throughout space and time. On the other hand, you will never incur karmic debt unless you need to incur it.

"Take a cooked chicken, for instance. What has happened to it? In most cases, the chicken knew what its fate would be, so it's okay to eat it. But then, there are a few chickens that did not know their fate, and by killing or eating a chicken that did not know its fate, you incur karma. So, you take your chances, and say a little prayer beforehand. But the vibration of karmic debt will come only to those who deserve it."

I sincerely hoped that I would never get a loaded chicken and become deathly ill. I thought of the ancient hunters and the Eskimos of today, who respect their kill and have reverence for the souls of the creatures that provide their sustenance.

"The karma that many steers go through is terribly painful," Hammal went on. "Many souls *choose* this road, as did a steer who was a bull in a former life and killed two people with his horns."

Hammal was not giving license for animal abuse of any kind, just stating the facts of this universe and how we choose our destinies. I thought of Gandhi who felt that you can gauge the evolution of a culture by the respect its animals are given.

Then Hammal shed light on another facet. "The minute you are born, you are trying to establish a direction relative to finding the truth of your nature," he began.

"Often, when a child becomes frustrated, it is due to his inability to find himself.

"Up to the age of seven, a child will carry traits from an earlier life, traces of the past, certain beauties from other lives and also certain problems. Mothers should learn to retain these truths for the child. And the child should be made aware of the beauty in himself or herself and in humankind.

"Children should not be ruled," he emphasized. "They should only be protected and guided. First and foremost, parents are to lead with kindness, light and strength. A teacher's direction—I refer to teacher in the universal sense; parents are teachers—is to realize the special nature of *each* individual and to realize the truth of each soul unfolding.

"Most mothers, however, break the wills of their children in order to make them more controllable. This is often part of a lesson for the child and, as I have stated before, mothers do not suffer karma for this.

"Every child who comes into the world has a few years in which he or she can change 20% of his or her vows and temperament. This can change every facet of his or her selected karmic path.

"Leah, for instance, changed her path by 2% when she decided that she would save *understanding* for another life. This kind of decision can be altered, but if it is, the debt will be more difficult to pay due to the vacillation from the original direction.

"Debt, I repeat, is something inherent in this universe and has to do with the development of the soul and a soul's responsibility to itself and to every other soul. Debt is not strictly incurred by wrongdoing.

"However, if a soul has wronged another soul, it has injured itself. The soul comes to understand what it has done through lessons. The individual learns why his or her beliefs are confused, careless, or out of line with individual evolution and thus the greater good. In this way, a debt must also be paid. But, as I have said, not all debts have to do with impropriety."

Hammal had answered my burning question: What exactly was confused and careless knowledge? Confused or careless knowledge was simply anything opposed to the truth of the soul, anything that prevented the soul from evolving, and hence the universe, from functioning as it should.

My mind flashed to an early episode of *Star Trek* in which the voyagers of the Starship Enterprise "beamed down" onto a mysterious planet. Unknown to them, it was a playground where each encountered an adventure that was based solely on the needs of the individual participating. One man met an old friend with whom he needed to resolve some long-standing issues. Another joyously met his late wife. A woman dressed in medieval garb encountered a knight on horseback. All were confused until they understood that they were in a intricately wired playground that responded to the subconscious needs of each participant. The voyagers, in fact, were creating their own situations and summoning their own images.

The earth is much the same, I thought—a playground for the soul with the adventures and physical encounters needed for a spiritual journey. Confused at first by the challenges encountered, eventually the soul's direction becomes clear and *care* is employed to maintain the truth of its individual journey and stay on its path to the light.

"Lessons are learned through *attachment,* Julia. There are things on the earth to be desired. And the things you desire the most in life are where your lessons will be learned.

"When you have worked through all that the earth has to offer you and you can respect, love, forgive, appreciate, and be kind and compassionate to yourself in all situations, then you can *release yourself* from the boundaries of the earth and future incarnations. For in the ability to love, forgive and respect yourself, you learn to love, forgive, respect and appreciate all souls. I cannot repeat this too often."

"The truth shall set you free," I thought to myself.

"The great minds, rulers and leaders on the earth plane are often master souls of other universes. They bring their light to this universe while they incarnate to work off their debt to the earth. When I speak of souls and debt in this way, I speak of *responsibility* to the universe, the cosmos, the entire Creation.

"The greater the light possessed by a soul, the greater their responsibility and the greater the debt owed to the universe as a whole. The debt of which I speak is a debt of love, just as a parent has a great responsibility to care for a child with love and kindness."

Hammal, then, focused on a closely related topic, one that put the bite into karma.

"The teacher of knowledge on the earth is pain," he asserted. "It is the way in which we are taught knowledge and truth. With each pain, the individual grows.

"In the same way that every soul works differently, pain is felt differently by every human being. One can never know anyone else's pain because everyone needs a different kind of teacher. We can only identify with someone else's pain through our own pain.

"The more evolved the soul, the deeper the pain, because the soul comprehends more. And the more that is realized with an understanding heart, the more compassion grows."

I flashed back to the time Havah and I had gone out for Chinese food. We were about to drive out of the restaurant parking lot when I eyed a small, scrawny shadow of a cat pulling scraps from the dumpster. Just seeing the cat and its circumstances gave me great pain.

I asked Hammal, "Why?"

Hammal answered, "Julia, you are suffering much more than the cat. This cat is at his own stage of evolution, learning what he needs to know. He feels nowhere near the pain you do in seeing him. Send him your light and love forever."

I understood that there were levels of learning for every soul, whether embodied in human or animal form. I also knew that Hammal was trying to comfort me because there was nothing I could physically do for the cat. He was semi-wild and mistrusting. I was already taking care of 4 dogs and 14 cats, two of which had been found near a dumpster. There was just so far my budget and the space in my house could stretch.

Then I remembered something that Hammal had told me earlier..."The beauty of a tattered stray or homeless being is generally unrecognized. However, no strays exist. No matter what their appearance, there is a purpose for each entity and a meaning in paths that have crossed. The secret is in recognizing why paths cross. Each soul is responsible for kindness to every other soul and we each have a responsibility to help in the development of every other soul."

He had also said, "Thought vibrations carry great weight."

Perhaps I saw the cat so that I could send him my love—a strong vibration of protection, love and healing. Perhaps the cat appeared so that I could comprehend, by example, that we all personally experience pain each in our own way.

Then I questioned, "Why poverty, starvation?"

"Everything that exists on the earth is here because it is needed. Poverty wouldn't exist if someone didn't need it," was his answer.

"Wars?"

"These are things inherent in the fabric of humanity. It has nothing to do with the soul," he replied.

"Often pain is self-inflicted," Hammal continued with his message. "Seventy percent of the time a soul gives pain to itself as a lesson in learning how to grow above it."

That was very interesting, I reflected. Seventy percent of the time, I give myself pain to challenge my growth.

"Through your physical body, you learn of pain. One of your first lessons in life is to learn to *feel.*

"All on the earth is pain, whether it is physical, emotional, deliberately inflicted or the result of extreme joy or frustration," he continued.

"On the soul level, all souls on earth experience pain. As I have said, if a stone has a soul, it will be compassionate to pain even though it does not experience actual physical pain. And pain is very closely related to fear. But I will talk more of this when we confer on grieving souls."

I considered the sensations felt by my body and the feelings of my heart. I thought again about the ultimate lesson of the earth—compassion, love, respect, forgiveness, appreciation—they were all *feelings.*

In the light of karma, Hammal reviewed how one follows currents and the responsibility of evolved souls.

"A higher level of communication brings with it greater responsibility," he reminded me. "The more you hear, the greater your accountability to your soul and the greater the rewards gained. Everything in the universe is connected; it is our limited vision, the facades, the veils, that keep us from really seeing.

"But currents are like debts to be paid," he continued. "When you feel the pull of a current, you are responsible to make some kind of commitment to it in order to fulfill your own life. Since you know there is something to be gained by following the current, you must follow it. This can be a most beautiful, fulfilling experience."

Karma, then, was also responsible for the creativity that resulted in my heightened feelings of euphoria, I reasoned, as well as the pain I experienced in seeing the cat scavenging in the dumpster.

"Everything has its own current, "Hammal repeated. "The pull of the currents has to do with the tug and the pull of the universe. They are related to resolution, to learning and to commitment. Those with greater vision have earned their vision by listening for more responsibility."

"When you 'ride' a current you are tied into the things that you need or the things that you can help," he reminded me. "You will not usually feel the pull of a current that doesn't go along with the tides of your own nature. This is why certain people attract, and are attracted to, similar things."

I thought over Hammal's message. There were things on the earth to be desired, gifts to be earned. Once I worked through that all the earth had to offer me and I could feel respect, love, forgiveness, appreciation, kindness and compassion for myself in all situations, I could release myself from the earth and future incarnations. Then, I would continue on to additional challenges in this, and other, universes.

But lessons here on the earth would be learned through attachments, karma and my response to the currents. The vibrations that I sent out would bring in my lessons. There was a price to be paid for lessons learned. And I had to accept payment for debts owed to me, as well.

I was required to allow the energy to flow from me and to me because giving and receiving are one in the same.

Karma, I thought, gives new meaning to the installment plan.

IV
Souls that Grieve

"Dearest Julia, disembodied souls are clogging the spherical forces around the earth. The airways have become so blocked, that although scheduled, no new light can be brought onto the planet.

"Masses of disembodied souls blanket many areas. These souls are in pain and do not know where to go or how to continue on.

"They are grouped together so closely that the negativity and fear in certain areas of the earth have resulted in many recent disasters. The situation is escalating to the point of even graver consequences.

"We of the Cosmic Angelic Force come to you for assistance in clearing the air." Hammal Cahone

Chapter 14

What is a Grieving Soul?
A Raniod? Illness?

"Dearest Julia, your soul is your truth, your direction—when you lose your truth, you lose your direction. You become lost and your soul grieves."

Hammal Cahone

Nikki, Tina, Aaron, Hairy and I were having a wonderful time playing catch. It was a four-ring circus—three black poodles, small, medium and large, plus one Yorkie.

Nikki reared like a small pony to catch the pink rubber squeaking porcupine. All twelve pounds of Tina Weena Jelly Beana dove under him after what looked like a miniature, taupe-colored hockey puck—the round corner of a Milk Bone that I had launched over the slippery tile floor—a game I called shuffle bone. Hairy the silvery-beige Yorkie barked, hot on her heels. And every time I laughed, Aaron stood up to dance and twirl on his hind legs.

My older cats sat rapt, watching the proceedings wide-eyed while the young cats flew through the hub of activity, joining in the fun and inventing their own games of bat the crumpled paper and hit the dog on the tail and run.

I laughed, tossed the squeak toy, launched the shuffle bone, twirled with Aaron and refereed the cats until I was exhausted.

"That's enough," I called over the yips and barks, and plopped down onto the bed. No one contested the decision, and we all settled down to watch TV while Tina gobbled up her shuffle bone.

We really gave the spherical forces a good workout, I chuckled to myself. Couldn't get much better in the good vibration department, either. I was blissfully relaxed when Hammal appeared.

"Dearest Julia," Hammal began with almost no warning. "A grieving soul is one that has either given up its body through shocking unexpected death, through confused knowledge, or in other ways that I will explain."

Finally! The book on the grieving souls was being opened—the last thing I expected on an effervescent evening. The contrast was jarring.

Hammal apologized for the interruption explaining that the air was very clear for the information, and it was of utmost importance that we begin.

He said that once the door was opened by this conference, it would be the first of many meetings on the grieving souls. Soon I would even be able to sit in on conversations with several of them.

How curious, I thought, and picked up the pad and pen that I had learned to keep close at hand.

"Up until now," Hammal continued, "I have been laying out the components of this universe as they apply to the incarnating soul. It is time to tell you what can happen to make a soul on the earth grieve and the consequences that can ensue.

"You know that each soul comes to the earth as a result of very careful planning—the energy must be right for the birth of each incarnating soul. You know that angels accompany the soul through the door of the physical plane to enter a body and become one with the earth; and a soul that has finished its work will be escorted from the earth with angelic protection as well.

"You understand that an incarnating soul has agreed to function in a body in order to fulfill its karma. And until that karma is fulfilled, the soul must remain on the earth.

"You are also aware that each soul is part of the spherical force and each body connects to the spherical force by way of the etheric body and the chakras. You realize all the angelic forces travel on the spherical force to bring in light, protection and healing to each individual. The spherical force is also your entre to, and exit from, the earth.

"I have told you that thought comes from the Universal Mind to be used creatively. And in order to keep the spherical forces moving around you, creative thought is necessary since the spherical forces will speed up or slow down according to your greater or lesser understanding or appreciation.

"You also comprehend that your soul is part of the Universal Soul. So your body is linked to your soul, the angelic forces, the Universal Mind, and the Universal Soul through the spherical forces.

"Now I will tell you that anything that causes you to completely lose the truth of your individual soul will *sever* your connection to your body.

"A body that has cut this connection has lost the map that tells it what to do, where to go and how to act on the earth. Separated from your direction, you will no longer be able to use your body to work out karma. *This* causes your soul to grieve.

"A soul may totally separate from its body before its time to leave the earth. If a soul gives up its body before it's time, it will become trapped on the earth or in the airways around the earth."

I thought back to the grieving masses and growing hordes of alienated, confused, lost souls that fly by day and night. They were torturing others and themselves and were responsible for the huge vortices and powerful cones of negative gravity that were sucking alien powers—gasses and viruses—onto the earth. These were souls that were supposed to be in bodies, but weren't. How desolate they must be. A cold chill filled the room.

"*Anything* that disrupts your soul's link to your body will cause your soul to grieve," Hammal emphasized.

"What would cause individuals to give up their souls?" I asked. But as I did, I remembered Hammal saying that the decision was made to give all souls a chance on the earth, many of whom were not sufficiently directed in their souls. I could hear him say: "When you add freedom of choice to lack of direction, in most individuals, utter confusion is created."

"To answer your question, Julia, a soul usually grieves because of careless, unclear or indirect knowledge from this life or from former lives," Hammal began to explain.

"This can occur as a result of ambitions gone awry or from fear, jealousy, weakness, or if a soul feels that it has been exploited. This misknowledge, this careless, unclear and indirect knowledge, distorts the soul's vision and injures the soul's ability to see.

"All souls have the ability to be beautiful," he added. "Most souls have a *vision* of beauty in them. Most, however, do not take advantage of this, allowing it to become lost or damaged.

"Even a highly evolved soul can become blinded and turn from the light, forgetting the understanding that he or she already has gained because of the intense pain felt."

I recalled Hammal saying that more evolved souls feel pain more deeply because the souls comprehend more. So evolution can work in reverse, I thought—a highly evolved soul may not be able to stand the pain it needs in order to grow.

"A soul can grieve because it doesn't know where to go through no fault of its own, as in the case of death by shock," Hammal continued. "Wars and violence create grieving souls because many are not scheduled for the traumatic deaths they experience.

"A soul can be born into a life as a grieving soul and can continue to grieve, helped along by family and circumstances.

"A fearful soul, who has known nothing but pain—who needs it until it can progress and grow beyond the need—may desire to be a grieving soul.

"A *true* grieving soul, however, is caused by karma. Tortured because of wrongs done in a former life or lives, the soul has no choice but to suffer in its own body.

"Otherwise, grieving is a *self-inflicted* condition, imposed by the souls themselves in the lives they are now leading.

"With few exceptions, whether or not to grieve is a decision that you as an individual make for yourself.

"There is a difference however between a grieving soul and a grieving heart—the mid-state is indecision.

"Many people blockade thought in an attempt to cloister themselves. In doing so, they slow down their spherical forces. This hinders a free flow of vibrations coming from the cosmos and causes many, many problems.

"If incoming thought, and new knowledge projected from the cosmic world, is blockaded and vibrations aren't accepted, an individual can't ride with them. So illness is created since the vibrations must break through in some way.

"Fevers, for instance, are often caused by blockades of hysteria—once the fever breaks, the blockade is opened.

"Sometimes a block may be sensed as a cold spot in or on the body. Usually caused by fear—as in *cold feet*—vibrations are hindered from flowing freely into the area.

"Most causes of cancer are the result of negative thought and negative vibrations. These vibrations must be cleared if one is to live."

Then Hammal began to explain something I had never heard of before, ranoids.

"Ranoids are fears in the auras that push out like bubbles," Hammal said, introducing the new concept.

"Once a ranoid is in the aura it becomes a living thing that draws energy out from the aura. It comes back at the individual with seven times the original force of the fear—the formula is equal to the amount of $fear^2$ times seven.

"For instance, if three ranoids are in an aura, the force will be sixty-three times the original fear, i.e., $(3^2 \times 7 = 63)$.

"Ranoid-like vibrations caused WW II. Grieving souls clustered over the area blocking it with too many vibrations. Even if good vibrations are in a blockaded area, one bad vibration can cause explosive events such as fits of rage, dogs chasing cats, cats chasing dogs—even war.

"The blockade contained the vibrations of fear and shot them forcefully back into the area to initiate WWII.

"This is much for you to digest for now. I will again take advantage of the weekend and we will continue tomorrow. Please hold your questions until then. Good night."

This was one night I didn't do too much thinking. The information seemed very clear. I decided to wait and see what news the morning would bring.

I readied myself for sleep and found that almost every furry body that could fit had beaten me to the bed. Gracefully draped over the pale pink, tulip-printed sheets, burrowed into the lime green blanket and nestled into the numerous pillows I kept for our mutual comfort, they slept like princes.

"Okay," I shouted, "everybody move over."

Tina and the cats quickly made room; but Hairy slept like a brick on his favorite pillow. Aaron reluctantly shifted, long enough for me to steal his head rest. Nikki figured he was set for the night—right in the middle of the bed. I wasn't about to argue.

So I found a pre-warmed spot at the foot of the king-size bed and fell asleep to the sound of the eleven o'clock news with Aaron sharing my pillow.

Chapter 15

Grieving Souls in the Auras

"Dearest Julia, What seers, or sensitives, have interpreted as holes or tears in the auras are, many times, disembodied grieving souls that 'sit' in the auras. The size of the hole depends on the kind of soul that has come." Hammal Cahone

Bamm! The doorknob slammed its imprint into the plaster wall. Another successful launch by Camber, my tortie-point Siamese, who had run full speed down the hallway to catapult off the open dining room door. My early wake-up call—Camber ruled the household and it was time for breakfast.

Boo, my one-eyed, anything-for-attention black cat scooted the empty, metal water bowl irritatingly across the tile floor. And the dogs, having heard a strange chain jingling outside, ran to the sliding glass door to bark obscenities at a four-legged intruder and nose-paint the clean glass.

Just another morning with the kids...I sleepily opened the back door. Nikki, Tina, Aaron, Hairy and three cats dashed into the yard to hastily inspect *their* property. Preoccupied with Hammal's lecture from the night before, I casually watched.

Hammal had extended the mind-body connection to the *body-soul* concept. In the light of his message, I began to equate illness as resistance to incoming cosmic knowledge from the Universal Mind.

Fear caused cold spots on the body, he said, and fevers were associated with hysteria. However, when a fever broke, the channels for incoming light were reopened. The idea that negativity created erratic movements in the spherical forces to cause even cancer was a totally new concept.

I mentally moved to the pain-fear connection and the human desire for status quo, mulling over the idea that we block knowledge because we are afraid of growing pains.

Illness would logically be the consequence of closed channels if you view the body as dense thought and equate even the tiny chakras in the blood as channels for incoming knowledge and healing.

I reviewed the common cold, flus and epidemics as the products of mass hysteria and group blockades.

I also reflected on the ranoids.

I considered the fearful, lost and grieving souls that huddled together to block the light. They were doing more than hindering angelic knowledge, protection and healing; they were instrumental in causing violence and brought in new diseases and gasses that added to our suffering.

Now Hammal and the angels were making this known so that humanity could help clear the air, allowing the scheduled new light from the Universal Mind to usher in the new age— the first circle of the next level.

We are the crucial generations, I thought to myself. It is up to us to save the earth and ourselves. I now knew more than ever that I, personally—I, beyond my extensions—had a pivotal role to play.

Hammal arrived to find me knee-deep in pet food, kitty litter and high hopes.

"Good morning, I see I'm a little early," Hammal was laughing. "Don't worry. This will be very brief."

Brief? Would this would be the morning I learned of my role? I was thrilled. But as Hammal settled into his discourse, I found the message was not what I had hoped it would be. "Patience, Julia," I calmed myself. "Hammal will tell you of your function when it is time."

"Dearest Julia, working within humankind's present knowledge, auric descriptions have been fairly accurate. But auric readers, although sensitive, are sometimes confused in what they see. However a new dimension will be understood today and an important inaccuracy will be corrected." Hammal was alerting me to an alarming aspect regarding the disembodied grieving souls.

"What seers, or sensitives, have interpreted as holes or tears in the auras are, many times, disembodied grieving souls that *sit* in the auras," he continued. "The size of the hole or holes depends on the kind of soul that has come. There can be more than one."

I listened with great interest since I had heard about entities in the auras from my teacher Lenore, an auric healer who could sense the presence of an intruder by the "drag" under her fingertips as she interpreted her complex, well-ordered charts.

"A grieving soul or souls that rides in the auras functions like space junk," Hammal continued. "Instead of moving spherically with the auras, their negative vibrations are sent out to impede or accelerate the movement of the spherical forces. This prevents the spherical forces from being receptive to the light. By blocking the lifeline of the host soul, these unwanted visitors cause the souls whose auras they inhabit to grieve. Herein lies a tremendous problem." Hammal paused.

This was critical information. Grieving souls not only grieved in their bodies, but once they gave up their bodies, they could fly into the tears or holes of another person's aura and cause them to become grieving souls as well.

143

"We of the Angelic Forces cannot continue with the proper placement of souls in the universe because within the auric system of some individuals, the kind, angelic forces are blocked."

I could see why Hammal waited to relay this message. The structure of the universe, the spherical forces (the delivery system of the incoming light) and the auras had to be clearly understood if the full implications were to be grasped. The entities didn't just cause illness, although that was bad enough. They were unwittingly creating more grieving souls as well.

Auric healers, believing that auras are merely torn, could seal in grieving souls that might otherwise be able to get free. Once trapped in the aura, a grieving soul or souls would cause the host to grieve. Even if a healer suspected that an entity was riding in an aura, he or she might still try to undertake repair, if not warned of the dangers.

"Healers," Hammal explained, "must ask the angelic forces if what they see are merely rips and tears *before* undertaking to mend auras. When grieving souls are riding in the aura, the healers must ask the angelic forces to *please remove the grieving souls and send them to their proper place.* Healers cannot undertake the removal personally. After the souls are removed, the auras can be sealed."

The picture grows worse, I thought—from the confused individual who blocks his or her own incoming light, to the lost and grieving souls that crowd the airways, to the disembodied grieving souls that jam the lifeline of an individual.

"How is an aura torn in the first place?" I asked.

"I will tell you this and much more this afternoon," Hammal replied. "I see you have a busy morning," he smiled and departed.

Camber sat purring, well-fed and satisfied, oblivious to the state of the earth. The dogs panted patiently at the back door, with visions of a cold tile floor in an air-conditioned house. And I turned to more immediate matters like preparing my own breakfast.

Chapter 16

How a Grieving Soul is Created

"Dearest Julia, grieving souls are created because people do not love themselves. Rather than fight, people are giving up their souls, the truth of their direction and the light." Hammal Cahone

Hammal made his opening statement, but I just couldn't identify. I loved myself. I loved my little family. And I was ready to fight for what I loved and believed in.

Besides, it was another brilliant, beautiful Miami afternoon and I was feeling great. No way could I ever think of giving up.

But as Hammal began to explain how an aura can be torn and how a soul can disembody, the information became more and more riveting. And I felt more and more vulnerable.

"An imbalance can be created in a moment of weakness, a second of doubt," he said.

A second of doubt? We all have moments of weakness, I thought.

"A weak spot can be inherited," said Hammal. "When one is born, a tiny part of a soul fragment is inherited from one's parents."

I was about to rationalize about luck and chance until I remembered that everything is planned out beforehand. There are no accidents.

"A mineral deficiency can cause a weak spot in earth-born souls—that is, souls that have originated on the earth as opposed to another universe," Hammal continued.

That was one I didn't have to worry about. Hammal had told me that I had come from elsewhere in the cosmos.

"You know the spherical forces (the major channels that link each individual to the universe) must be in balance to receive a free flow of creative, life-sustaining energy," Hammal went on. "But the spherical forces cannot be in balance if the energy in the physical body and the chakras are out of balance.

"Even if the chakras, the energy, and the physical body are in balance, an imbalance can still exist in the spherical forces. Things can go wrong when the auric force closest to the physical body is not centered. When this occurs, there is an imbalance in the entire auric system."

Recalling that the auric force nearest the body was a polarized force with a north and south axis, I suddenly remembered that the earth was off of its axis. I had heard that the earth's axis was moving farther from center yearly. Was this another indication of the events that threatened?

Hammal continued, "The imbalance in the auric system can be brought about by atmospheric conditions that can generate blockages in the spherical forces."

Atmospheric conditions? He definitely had my attention now. This was something totally beyond my control.

"And, as I've already told you, careless knowledge from this life or from former lives, an imbalance induced by fear, jealousy, ambition, weakness, and exploitation, or the intensity of pain in a highly evolved soul that causes the soul to become blinded can result in a grieving soul. There are other reasons as well.

"But once an individual's auric force is off-balance, the spherical forces go out of balance too. With the vibrations out of sync, there can be no exchange between the soul and the cosmic forces. This precipitates a greater imbalance.

"When the imbalance becomes too great, the auric force can spill out, increasing the possibility of incurring a weak spot where none existed; and an existing weak spot or spots can become holes.

"It takes only one weak spot to weaken your entire spherical force," he emphasized. "And a hole in an aura can induce even greater debility—it is an invitation for disembodied grieving souls or a soul fragment to enter.

"When a disembodied soul enters, friction is set up by the alien vibration. This slows down or speeds up the spherical force, which creates negativity and shock waves. These increasingly weaken the aura and the spherical forces of the host.

"At first the grieving souls can move in and out of the host's aura. But when light and the angelic forces can no longer penetrate the spherical forces around the host, the disembodied souls become locked in—on rare occasions they are accidently sealed in by auric healers as I have told you before.

"Once locked in, the disembodied souls are forced closer and closer to the physical body of the host because the spherical forces can no longer allow them to leave.

"Now the soul of the *host* begins to go in and out of its own body since there is no longer any strength or basic truth left to hold it. Increasing weakness is noted. Fatal skin diseases, life-threatening cancers and diseases can result.

"At some point, the host could vacate his or her own body entirely to become another disembodied grieving soul.

"If the host soul disembodies, it could try to live on in another body that has no soul—one that has been vacated by another individual who has also given up.

"If a host's original body dies, the disembodied soul can still continue to live on in its 'selected' body.

"But if a disembodied soul tries to return to its original body once that body has died, it obviously cannot. So the lost soul must find a new vehicle that has been vacated, oust a weaker soul from a residence it has taken over, or look for an aura with a hole in it and make that its home."

I listened, petrified.

"If the original body of the host is still alive," Hammal continued, "a soul from another vacated shell can take over that body totally, unless a stronger one comes along to force it out or unless the original soul returns."

This gives new meaning to the shell game, I thought, picturing a carnival character with his slight of hand. Under which shell is the pea? In which body is the original soul? But the stakes were much, much higher.

"A vampire fragment can also take over while the original soul is out of its shell—yes, Julia, they exist on a soul level."

"What is a vampire fragment?" I wanted to know. This whole scenario was terrifying enough without the added visions I was imagining.

"I will tell you more about this later. Just remember that nothing comes to you that you do not invite or that isn't part of your karma."

Hammal continued with his scheduled material.

"You don't have to be a grieving soul in order to host a disembodied grieving soul," Hammal said. "A disembodied grieving soul can enter into a hole that is the result of a shock or injury to the body of the host. It can occur from physical weakness."

Later I found out that a vampire soul could also tear a hole in an aura.

"As explained..." Hammal continued to unfold the information, "...a grieving soul can disembody prematurely as the result of a surprise death or a soul can leave its body without knowing where it is to go.

"And, you already realize that a soul can disembody because it has grieved on its own while embodied: finally the body sends the soul away."

I was totally overwhelmed. But there was still more...

"A grieving disembodied soul can be an animal or a devic entity, a rock, or a nature spirit, such as water or tree spirit that attracts pure thought and positive energy. If one of these enters an animal of a radically different vibration, the animal will appear crazed and die because the vibration is so foreign. This does not account for all cases of madness, however.

"Do you have any questions?" he asked.

I was dumbfounded.

I told Hammal that I had to think everything over. I needed distance from the material to allow it settle in slowly. Hammal agreed to return the next day, Sunday morning.

I had much to think over and an exciting Saturday night to prepare for. Love was in blossom, as it had been for many years. I was looking forward to attending an art opening with the man I told you about earlier—a brilliant, charismatic artist with a beautiful soul. I had searched for him from the moment I was born.

We had met with a passionate clash of wills—"thunderbolts," said a Latin acquaintance who witnessed the event incredulously. Everyone who came near us felt the overwhelming electrical surges as two high-tension wires made all their vital connections.

Whenever we would enter a restaurant or any room, large or small, light bulbs flickered, popped and burned out. The air around us crackled. We laughed and watched to see how many lights would surrender to us as we entered.

In the first week, I wrote a verse that he carried in his wallet until it was almost illegible. And then, he continued to carry it.

Bodies break,
Bump,
Bind.
Spirits soar,
Sail,
Sing,
Permeate each vital thing,
Embrace the sun,
Breathe the wind
And love the soil—Creativity's spring.

No miles,
No bounds inhibit souls.
They are—
Alive.

Our life together was just that—alive. We could feel each
other's heart beat and lungs expand over thousands of miles of
physical separation. I would know whenever he was ill. And
after we had finally parted, I would writhe in psychic pain
whenever he gave up one of his auras or another piece of his
soul. Eventually he gave up his soul.

I can never describe the heights of ecstasy or the bitter-
sweet pain of our fifteen-year relationship. It would finally
reveal that all my love, my will, and my determination wasn't
enough to save him.

I would often recall Hammal's words: "The intensity of
pain in a highly evolved soul can cause the soul to become
blinded. It was up to the individual soul to keep its direction."

But for the moment my heart sang and my soul soared.
Our eyes were about to meet, our bodies would touch, we
would inhale each other's presence, leave the earth and travel
on the light over the spherical forces together. The evening held
the promise of exquisite excitement and adventure.

When I arrived home, Nikki, Tina and the gang greeted me with the fury of their joy amidst furry hugs and juicy kisses. I settled in, grounding myself long enough to review the notes from the morning's conference and make a quick summary of the complex material. I noted:

The creation of a grieving soul begins when the imbalance of a soul becomes too great and the strength in the spherical forces decreases until it is too difficult for the soul to see the light. Confusion and impure knowledge can then infiltrate, and weak spots and holes can occur in the aura.

As the weakness becomes greater, disembodied grieving souls can enter into the holes. The alien souls can also be the souls of trees, animals, rocks, devic or nature spirits, vampire spirits and others.

The disembodied grieving "rider" souls become like space junk with alien vibrations that slow down or speed up the vibrations of the host. They set off shock waves to cause erratic movements within the spherical forces.

With increased weakness in the spherical forces, the host soul begins to travel in and out of its own body until it leaves its body altogether.

The former host, now a grieving disembodied soul, looks for an aura with a hole or another shell (vacated body) to inhabit.

The questions started to come.

How can you know if you are born of the earth? And if you don't know, shouldn't you insure the strength of your aura by taking in minerals?

What kind of auric disturbances cause the spherical forces to misalign?

Were my thoughts about the earth's axis correct?

How can people love themselves more?

What can you do if you inherit a weak spot?

How do you know if your aura has a tear?

How do you know if there is a grieving soul or souls already in your aura?

If there is a disembodied soul in your aura, how can you get rid of it?

And I wanted to know about the vampire fragment, the nature spirits and extreme vibrations, and how they could enter the aura of a foreign entity.

My dreams that night were a curious mix of sugar plums and disembodied spirits—much like my relationship with my lover in the years to come.

Chapter 17

Conversations with Grieving Souls

"Dearest Julia, There are actual grieving souls that inhabit their own bodies. There are disembodied grieving souls that sit in auras and those that hang out in the spherical forces and block the airwaves. Then there are the takeovers—those who are disembodied grieving souls that have found another empty shell in which to reside, a body that has been vacated by another soul." Hammal Cahone

Morning had come and gone. Hammal appeared briefly to say that our plans for the scheduled meeting had changed. He asked me to call Leah, a close friend who knew of our work, and invite her to the meeting he set for 7 p.m. Then he was off "to wind the clock" somewhere.

The sunny Sunday slowly succumbed to twilight. Biscayne Bay flashed incandescent as the coconut palms silhouetted, postcard perfect, against the red and orange streaked sky.

It was still light when Leah arrived.

She was stunning—long and lean with raven hair and doe-eyes, her skin tanned a deep, dark bronze.

Hammal had explained to me that Leah was a powerful vibration who could open up her cosmic extensions if she came to grips with a problem she was having. She was an embodied grieving soul, he said. She no longer is.

Hammal greeted us both and told Leah that he was pleased she could come. He commenced the conference as darkness quickly fell.

"*Actual* grieving souls are lost souls that grieve while in their own bodies." He began to list the various categories of grieving souls.

"The disembodied grieving souls that I have spoken of at length that enter through a hole and sit in the auras of embodied souls are known as *riders.*

"*Hangers out* are disembodied grieving souls that hang out in the airways, or spherical forces, and block the light. As souls without a vehicle (shell or body) they are very pained, as are the lost souls on the earth.

"*Takeovers* are disembodied grieving souls that have found a shell, or another body, in which to reside. They may or may not remain in the body they have taken over. The original soul may return to claim its body or a stronger disembodied soul may oust the weaker soul. Fights can ensue."

Hammal began to expound. "Life as a rider grieving soul is quite uncomfortable," he said. "Along with making the host it rides uneasy, the rider feels boxed in.

"In searching for a permanent body, the rider has found a false refuge which gives it no pleasure. This soul is generally a seeker who longs for freedom. The soul is looking for an answer and is aware of its pain.

"Once inside the aura, however, the soul has no control over itself; on occasion certain elements of its character combine with the soul that is being ridden. Some of its compulsions combine with the soul it rides and frustrations abound from its unfulfilled needs. The rider is not allowed to leave until the time is right, which happens very infrequently.

"If there is a shock to the individual being ridden, this could open up a channel of escape. Meanwhile, the rider will try to fulfill its existence through the host soul without any success. So the soul that connects itself to another soul is in desperate condition. The rider becomes even sadder, and the weight of the rider feeds off of the host.

"These souls could be broken apart by shock, as I mentioned. They also can be separated if the individual being ridden is a believer in deep prayer. But how many people will know that they have an extra soul hanging on? Herein lies the problem."

One of my questions was answered. How many of us even question if an extra soul is hanging on to us?

Then Hammal surprised me by saying, "We are going to talk to a soul who is in an aura. His name is Samuel."

Aside from my introductions to the heads of Hammal's cabinet, this was the first conversation I was a party to.

I will recount the brief conversation exactly as it happened.

Samuel: "Hello, I'm unhappy."

Hammal: "Why?"

Samuel: "I feel like a prisoner."

"How did he get there?" I asked Hammal.

"He died unexpectedly and didn't believe that he was dead. He still doesn't believe that he is dead. So he's looking for the truth. He found an open space in an aura and has been in there for two-and-a-half years."

"Why doesn't he believe he's dead?"

"Because he's supposed to have lived for eight more years. He died suddenly when a brick accidentally fell on his head. Now he's attached himself to the aura of a young woman who is herself a grieving soul. Her spherical force is very tacky. It has attracted eight grieving souls who are at present taking up residence in her auras," Hammal responded.

"I thought that there were no accidents," I was puzzled.

"There aren't, Julia, He just wasn't expecting to die at that time and in that manner. Some unfinished karma from a former life caught up with him. This can happen to anyone."

That was the only conversation with Samuel. I didn't think to question the possible esoteric significance of the eight years or the eight grieving souls. In retrospect, I don't believe that there was any...or was there?

Following this, I was introduced to another soul that was hanging out in the airwaves.

"This soul has been hanging out in the sky for 1500 years," Hammal explained. "His name is Jehovah and he hates being in the sky. His chains don't move. He doesn't know where to go at all.

"He wasn't born on this planet; even so, he came to the earth and believes that he is where he is supposed to be. He *was* scheduled to be here but was late. His mother, who lived near Syria, had a miscarriage when she was kicked in the stomach by a donkey 3008 years ago.

"He is not the person that you are thinking of, but he has been a seer in the Holy Land and in Europe. He has been here on the earth twelve times."

"How did he get into the sky this time?"

"He was semi-crucified," Hammal replied. "People thought that he was crazy. He died, but his soul left his body before he physically died; so he doesn't believe that anything happened. He has almost total amnesia of his lives.

"He is over Chicago now but he drifts. Even if he stays in the same place, the earth rotates. He knows that he's got problems but doesn't know how great they are.

"The power of the mind is a tremendous thing. You can forget everything to make the pain less."

I didn't get to talk with Jehovah personally although I was transported to the place where he was bound.

Then Hammal turned to Leah. This conversation, too, is as it occurred.

Hammal: "Did you talk to J—— about creative thinking?"

Leah: "No."

Hammal: "Why?"

Leah: "I'm not thinking, I have this pain, this problem. I think, maybe, it's because I'm not where I want to be."

Hammal: "No, it's not because of that. The pain comes from only one thing, lack of appreciation. Appreciation has many subdivisions. Taking things for granted is one. Thinking negatively about something is another.

"You have thought this way all of your life and you have to work this out. That's why you have the pain.

"You feel cheated because you can't get the things you want. You are hostile. It's part of appreciation—to think creatively means that you are thinking out of love and concern.

"If you feel deprived, you can't achieve what you want to achieve. You could work something out through hostility but that would never last.

"You don't have that many things to do and you could organize better. You have to start making more decisions on your own.

"You would like people to tell you what to do, then try to do it. If things don't work out the way you want them to, you resent it.

"You have not been saying 'thank you' and appreciating. Remind yourself in your thoughts.

"Why do you feel defensive already? I'm talking to you out of love. If you feel defensive you won't hear what is said. You will just send out vibes that will make someone else feel unwell and make you feel sick.

"What did I say?"

Leah: "I'm supposed to say thank you. I'm supposed to say thank you because people are..."

Hammal: "No, that's not what was said. You have to train

yourself not to feel cheated because you are very lucky. But you kill yourself with your attitude. That is the problem. And this results in a lack of appreciation. You feel hostile to everyone, and to yourself. You don't reach out and direct your thinking.

"Take your friend, for instance. You want him to decide certain things. He can try to help, but it's not his fault if it doesn't happen. It's not anyone's fault. You want him to tell you exactly what to do and then you blame him if you don't do it.

"We hope you can work creatively. You make the direction yourself. If you want to be hand fed, you'll always be cheated. You have to go for it. You have to send the vibration out by searching.

"Yes, things come to you when they are supposed to, but only if you set the vibration. This is part of creative thought. Now we hope to have planted a new seed.

"You have to understand that you are a strong vibration. Everything that you have has been given to you as a gift so that you can use it to the best possible purpose. And that's all!

"When you continually dredge up the past, you set the vibrations all over again. You relive it. That vibration will exist and continue to hurt you.

"Now what did I say?"

Leah: "I should learn not to feel cheated and that way I won't be hostile. I should make decisions more."

Hammal: "Why?"

Leah: "So it... life... won't be so boring."

Hammal: "No. You should not give the responsibility of making the decision to anyone. The only one who can cheat you is you. Everyone is going through painful experiences at the same time that you are and sometimes it is hard for them to see what you need.

"Pain is eight times greater if you keep repeating it from the past. Telling you this is a gift. Get the pain out for a second;

get it out and go on. The pain is of your own making.

Leah: "Am I taking things for granted?"

Hammal: "Yes. It all goes hand in hand. Do you know what taking things for granted is?"

Leah: "Yeah, things are just there."

Hammal: "They're really not there. Any minute they will be taken away. Once you realize that, you will understand.

"What is love? It's the touching of souls. If you touch (live in) the past, you can't send out a vibration to another soul. It should make you happy to know that. It's a key for you and your happiness. If you look with an open soul, you will find what you are looking for. But if you look when your soul is full of the past, you will never find.

"What pains you so?"

Leah: "I can't give it up yet. I have nothing to put in there."

Hammal: "Why don't you work with yourself more, get a better understanding and make yourself happy? Why can't you let yourself be happy?"

Leah: "I don't want to be here."

Hammal: "So you feel cheated."

Leah: "No, I just don't want to be here."

Hammal: "That's really too bad. Nobody wants to be here. J—— has to struggle everyday. Your friend has to struggle. There are a lot of beautiful things here to appreciate and that's what you have to do. You are so beautiful and so kind—it's important that you really look at yourself with the words I've just said.

"You have to find your own way or you are going to ruin yourself. You'll have to come back to the earth many more times.

"You should give people more chances than you give them. That's part of appreciation and loving. It's part of forgiving. You can't live in the past; you must find your own happiness. I know it was difficult to leave your mother country. I also understand. I lost my Shangri-la. But the beauty will live with you all of your life.

"You're being protected because you are very valuable. You don't believe it? Maybe you're taking yourself for granted too. It's not so rough here."

Leah: "I don't like it."

Hammal: "I don't like it either but make the best of it. Always look for something to love in what you do; you will find it. Eventually it will be second nature."

Leah: "It's real and it's unreal..."

Hammal: "Its unreal and it's real but you make the best of it. Remember these words and study them. It's the answer to all of your problems. It's a gift.

"We do live out certain things through our physical body. You are sensitive enough to know this. We play. We work. It's all part of loving. It's the key to your problem—all of your problems.

"Read these notes because it's your way of studying. It's good for you. It works; it's your way to work. Read the material every two days."

Hammal left us both with these words: "The important thing to remember about grieving souls is that every grieving soul is a part of all souls. This means that every grieving soul is a part of you. As long as there are grieving souls, we shall all be grieving."

Leah and I were quiet for some time. We both thought over the evening's message.

Our souls were being nourished but our stomachs began to grumble from neglect.

It was still early in the evening. We phoned my sister and Havah. No one had eaten so we all met for Thai food. The hot and spicy Sea Food Supreme with a cold glass of St. Pauli Girl quickly brought us back to earth.

Chapter 18

Physical Aspects, Water and Vortices

"Dearest Julia, A grieving soul can be seen as friendly and warm one day, and not the next."

Hammal Cahone

I had been at the studio, drawing a series of very strange images—multi-petalled flowers whipped in whirlwinds around static faces of children who stared numbly from the centers and flat, floral masks—torn, red anthuriums with frightened human eyes that peered out through the holes. The images were fascinating, but I had no idea of their meaning until Hammal delivered the following lecture.

"When a grieving soul or souls have entered into the spherical forces of another grieving soul, fearful eyes seem to peer out as if from behind a mask—the eyes appearing about two inches behind the mask."

Hammal paused to address me personally, "Julia the pastels you have been sketching are images of grieving souls. We thank you for them, and also for bringing in Pegasus and the three stages of cosmic travel."

Riveted by the symbolic drawings that seemed to appear on their own to illuminate the paper, *The Three Stages of Travel* showed my profile as an extension of a brilliant red,

white and black butterfly-wing that resembled a headdress—
the image was repeated in three different positions, one over-
lapping the other. The serene profile tilted farther and farther
backwards into the spherical forces, illustrating humanity's
progression to cosmic flight.

Pegasus flew from sheets of colored rice paper, drawn in
pen, ink, colored pencil, pastel and gilt. In my jewelry designs,
he hovered in an acrylic box suspended on a golden chain—a
three-dimensional 18-karat miniature.

Mysterious sketches would sometimes include seven
winged spheres along with a free-flying Pegasus reflected in
the seventh sphere. Variations included surreal, four-foot high
Alice in Wonderland type playing cards. Still others illustrated
a diminutive, flying steed soaring as music, trumpeted from the
throat of a flower. One image was accompanied by a verse.

> There is a land of magic and mist,
> of dreaming and sleeping,
> and soft, silent stirrings,
> where creatures with wings
> live in the flowers that trumpet their going.
> Pegasus was from such a world.
> The flowers still sound
> of his leaving.

Pegasus was elation; the drawings of the grieving souls
were disconcerting and provocative.

"There is an absence of color in the skin," Hammal re-
sumed his description of a grieving soul. "Fists may be
clenched or there may be an opening and closing of the fists.
And body vitality is usually low due to the energy expended in
grieving.

"These traits are also reflected in a shell that has been
taken over by another grieving soul. And once a grieving soul

has entered a body other than its own, the entered vehicle is also generally low in vitality.

"A grieving soul may vomit a great deal once it takes over a shell or when the original embodied grieving soul becomes weakened. This happens in both cases because the vibrations are wrong for the souls.

"The grieving soul or souls that are foreign to the shell can move in and out of the body and the spherical forces. But if they become locked in, as I have told you before, such havoc is caused in the vibrations that diseases such as cancer and tuber-culosis occur, and incurable skin eruptions that will eventually kill the individual.

"Even though the original soul has left its body, a cell memory remains. This is a memory of what was. The soul no longer incurs karma through that body because the original soul no longer has the ability to do harm through it—if that was its orientation. It is possible however for some karma to be worked off through the shell.

"When a soul has gone, the etheric double will have the appearance of what the soul has been. An uninhabited body can live up to seven years, functioning from the cell memory.

"Should a stronger entity intrude, there will be a physical change after three months. If the intruder is less powerful, then little things such as attitudes will change."

For days after Hammal's description, I could see grieving souls in people walking on the street, visiting the studio and in people I knew. I'm sure my perceptions were heightened by the angels so that I could actually see what Hammal was talking about. Once I was open to the images, they were everywhere.

Hammal took a brief break while the airwaves cleared so another aspect of the information could be channeled—griev-ing souls and bodies of water.

"Grieving disembodied souls that hover above the water do not normally latch onto other souls since there are usually none to grab onto. And because the souls cannot travel through the water, these souls are lost.

"Occasionally, a grieving disembodied soul will try to find its way via the water—one soul has tried to work through an octopus for the past eight years. This is causing problems since the soul is used to only two arms, et cetera."

I chuckled to myself, visualizing the picture. I sometimes have trouble using two arms, but eight.... It must be terrifying for the soul, I thought.

"Grieving embodied souls that remain near water will dry out, "Hammal disclosed. "Purified by the water, the souls will no longer grieve and can continue on."

What a wonderful bit of information. I wondered if that's why I have always needed to live near water. Perhaps some innate sense of protection was directing me.

"Have you ever studied sailors and those who work with the sea?" Hammal asked. "They become part of it. A cleansing takes place that carries them far, far away—much like meditation. When you are on the water, there is no other way to look at yourself except in relation to the universe. In doing so, you forget yourself."

Another clue for protection. I made a note.

"If a disembodied grieving soul has latched onto a body and wants to be released from that body, it cannot be accomplished over the water because a balance is maintained by the basic elements: the salt of the sea, the earth (the bed) of the sea, and the water of the water. Unless some kind of cosmic force overpowers this balance, such as in The Devil's Triangle, the soul cannot be released.

"Since a lost, disembodied soul is generally looking for a vehicle (a body, a shell, a weakened aura), it will tend to drift more toward land where it can manifest."

More information about the whirlwinds, the negative vortices, was about to come.

"Disembodied souls can group together, causing huge funnels of negativity," the message started. "These cones, or vortices, are the result of pulls by the grieving soul population. The power of a cone draws the grieving souls up like a tornado, or funnel cloud, while sucking other negativity down onto the earth. The earth becomes unbalanced from the negative gravity pulls. Similar in nature to pyramid power in that the funnels can draw foreign elements onto the earth. But the elements being drawn in are negative. They are disease and chaos, as I have disclosed before. This is a tremendous problem for the earth.

"When the cones have gotten too full and the negative energy gets too strong, the cones burst and grieving souls are sent flying into the solar system. This is another big problem. It is one way of getting rid of the cones, but it clogs up the entire solar system.

On a physical level, the bursting cones cause radical changes—eruptions, earthquakes, tidal waves and undercurrents are sent out. Grieving souls riding in auras are greatly affected. People become nervous. Weaknesses—from personal to planetary—are amplified.

"And with the violent events that result, more grieving souls are created by death through shock. These, too, add to the blockages in the light."

Another big bite of information. The situation was overwhelming—an immense cycle of negativity was totally out of hand.

Again I thought of Hammal's earlier message: "The earth is again returning to the seventh circle to gain new knowledge. We do not have to be destroyed if we can go back to the knowledge we once had in the last seven circles and relearn the positive aspects. If we can keep the human race intact without destruction, then we can come back and travel on the light into the cosmos, while humanity is still embodied on earth in the seventh circle."

The challenge was colossal but not hopeless.

Hammal's earlier messages echoed in my mind: "We of the Cosmic Angelic Force are trying to *repair* humankind's thoughts and allow humanity to be *free*. Mankind would learn faster if there were *no* grieving souls to block the light."

I also realized that we, embodied as we are now on the earth, would never realize eight, the evolution of the earth when debt would be dead and heaven would exist on this earth.

We were just entering the seventh circle. It was up to us to make "eight" a reality for generations to come—generations in which our souls would participate, incarnated as our own progeny.

My drawings of the grieving souls illustrated the situation that exists on earth now; the whirlwinds symbolized the spherical forces. Pegasus was hope, the day when humanity while still in physical form could take spiritual flight from this planet into the cosmos. And the *Three Stages of Travel* illustrated the progression of humanity.

I didn't want to think about the alternative. I had seen too many vivid imaginations project the downward spirals on TV and movie screens.

I really needed to know more about "the plan."

Chapter 19
A World of Opposites, Vampires, Impure Yellow

"Dearest Julia, With negativity, the earth will destruct; with positivity it will evolve into the light."

Hammal Cahone

I didn't think the incoming messages could get more frightening but they did as Hammal emphasized the importance of protecting one's soul.

Although Hammal had said that hell did not exist, I thought that if it did we were living right in the middle of it.

"Dearest Julia, the earth, as you know, is a place of polarity with light and dark, good and evil," Hammal began. "This does not exist cosmically. Opposites exist only in the visible, physical world. Cosmically there is no direct opposition. For us, the angelic forces, there is only greater or lesser."

"Is there any place more negative than the earth?" I finally asked a question I had held back for a long time. I really believed that the earth was hell and it was only up from here.

"There are planets darker than the earth because there is no light—light being the angelic forces. Negative, however, is not used outside of the earth, not even as an electrical term. The words 'force' and 'energy' are used," he explained, "greater and lesser directed force or energy."

"Do we have to go to those darker places in order to learn?" I cringed in anticipation of the answer.

"The other planets are a choice and do not have to be worked through as the earth," he answered. "One lifetime is usually enough and it saves you time when you come to the earth."

Well at least there was an up side, I thought.

Having answered my questions, Hammal continued with his information. "In the cosmos there are *mirrored reflections* rather than positive and negative. As I said, we do not talk of good and evil.

"In terms of color, the highest good is gold. Yellow of lesser clarity reflects muddled or impure thought. So from a cosmic viewpoint, *impure yellow* is lesser gold. Recognition of this makes it a reality. But it is only a reality on this planet."

Hammal was saying impure yellow was equal to the most negative ill intentions—the most impure yellow is what we might call evil on the earth.

"When a soul goes out of balance in the extreme, impure yellow (confused or muddled thinking) directs itself to the soul."

Hammal stopped the incoming message to emphatically announce, "I want you, Julia, to remind all of humanity of the importance of prayer."

That said, he continued. "People with impure yellow entities cannot call in the angelic forces since they cannot balance their vibrations in order to allow in truth. But they *can* invite other grieving souls that share a similar negative tone or vibration, or those who have a like negative aspect about them, into their lives and into their auras. Entities with sufficient force can eventually take them over. This is *exactly* what happens.

"To be receptive to the truth," he explained, "a soul has to be willing to purify itself and incorporate the vibration of truth into its existence because everything works on vibrations. You will call in what you project. Truth attracts truth, the angelic forces, and the light. Confusion, unclear knowledge, carelessness about your life and your direction will bring in grief.

"Angles are always here and ready to help," Hammal spoke with great love, "but they *cannot* because the impure yellow entities have their own force on this planet and can take the place of angels in the auras."

I pictured the spherical forces, the envelopes of thought energy.

Hammal had said, "See yourself as part of a whole system of energy—part of a package, or compression, that lines up against interior walls made solely of thought—wall, upon wall, upon wall of thought, ad infinitum. These walls of thought surround each and every individual."

I remembered that creative thought drove the entire spherical force.

"Greater or lesser energy," Hammal had said, "was created by greater or lesser *understanding*."

I pictured the whirring energy envelopes being fed by thought, energy envelopes that were thought themselves—layer upon layer of creative thoughts linking with higher and higher knowledge, truth and light.

I remembered Hammal saying, "Simplified, directed and disciplined thought generates greater or lesser spherical force. Most often the walls repress or depress the outer regions of cosmic energy, inhibiting new thought."

So this was the full meaning of repressed and depressed outer regions of cosmic energy. Hammal was saying that the vibration of the angelic forces couldn't penetrate the spherical forces around an individual who did not have sufficient discipline, appreciation, understanding or speed to participate in the incoming the light. The person had indulged in impure yellow thoughts or careless knowledge. He or she may have even attracted impure yellow entities, possibly vampires, into his or her circle of acquaintances and ultimately into their auras. All of the above can exist simultaneously.

"Friction is set up between the grieving souls, the impure yellow entities and the truth of the soul—the truth of the soul is previous knowledge that exists on an unconscious level," Hammal continued to explain. "So the motion of the spherical forces becomes such that the angelic forces, who are kind and want to help, are pushed to the outer edges of the auras.

"Even though they try to get into the auras to clear the grieving souls, the angelic forces are prevented by the friction set up by erratic vibrations.

"The friction will sometimes ignite a spark that causes the spherical forces to move faster. This is hurried on by the individual's brain which is in a sense of confusion."

Hammal began to illustrate what can happen to the auras and the spherical forces by listing my various students and various acquaintances.

"You know Michael Keeper. He has eight grieving souls and four impure yellow entities in his aura. Mass confusion exists. If you have noticed, he very frequently has a red face.

"Leah's friend Uri has been open to impure yellow since Leah left her homeland. He desires to do good but has not developed his thought process enough to move his soul. His auras are blockaded, just as the auras of humanity are blockaded. His spherical forces are almost motionless—a directed nothing to nowhere. This is all right, but not for anyone he touches.

"Barbara Flowers has bad thoughts and can't be helped right now.

"Harold does not want to be helped.

"There are embodied souls with vampire qualities," Hammal expounded. "And when two vampire vibrations are present in the same room, much damage is caused to the souls around them.

170

"By themselves, vampires can rip open an aura and place a vampire fragment into it, causing a soul that was formerly not grieving to grieve. This is why I tell you that it is very important to constantly pray for protection and guard your aura. Anyone whose hunger is too strong to be contained can become a vampire spirit.

"Frank's soul almost completely left, letting a vampire spirit in. In his case it was a general vampire spirit which is not sent by an individual. His wife has been a vampire spirit, time and time again. She is no longer herself but is a vampire. Janet Jefferson is also a general vampire spirit.

"One who is very close to you has two weak spots in her auras. One is in the astral aura—this is because she is hungry and desirous of things that do not belong to her in this life. The other spot occurred because the spherical force was slowed down by muddled thought. She deliberately causes her own confusion and needs to think more clearly. A vampire can send a grieving soul into these holes. Although she will have no contact with a vampire in this life, serious illness is possible unless her thinking is revised.

"Your friend Carol has a high probability of being consumed. She is being eaten away at.

"Gloria Bambini left her body four months and three weeks ago. Her soul left because of weakness, selfishness and hatred. Her mother, an actual vampire soul, finally took over Gloria's body. Gloria always fought it but she finally gave in. The person you know is no longer Gloria. Death awaits her— impure yellow directed by black forces eats away at the truth. She, too, has been a vampire in a former life."

I was shocked. These are just people that you would meet anywhere, at a neighborhood barbecue, at the movies, in the supermarket. But this is the state of humanity and the earth.

I was somewhat relieved when Hammal explained, "Impure yellow is a force that stays on this planet. And individuals who entertain impure forces cannot leave the earth until they are rid of it. Along with karma and debt, it is a major lesson of this planet." Hammal confided.

"A d_ _ _ _ _ic entity," Hammal would not use the word for fear of calling in the force, "is created when a vacated vehicle (body, shell) has been taken over by the most base, aggressive black forces.

"If a grieving soul moves out of its body and the body is taken over by a d_ _ _ _ _ ic entity, it will last only eight years on its own energy. But if the original soul moves in and out of its body, it can last an indefinite amount of time.

"D_ _ _ _ ic grieving souls can rip holes in auras and get in. They wait for a weak moment. A second will do. The act is sometimes karmic. Usually this entity will rip the auras of people it has known, trying to get even with a person for the harm that the entity thinks occurred; in reality it may or may not have occurred. If the soul that the d_ _ _ _ ic entity is trying to harm is too strong, the entity will go to someone the person loves and cause injury and pain in a roundabout way."

The descriptions were terrifying.

"We will teach you how to protect your soul and those you love. We will also teach you how to pray for the earth."

Chapter 20

Does it Matter if the Earth Destructs?

"Dearest Julia, The earth was not made to be destroyed." Hammal Cahone

I now more than anxiously awaited "the plan" as Hammal quickly convened another conference to clear up any doubt relative to the earth and the souls that had committed themselves to learning here.

"Humanity causes the destruction of the human race and also of the planet on which it resides." He began to recap the situation and the possible outcome of the seventh circle.

"The earth has a soul that is affected by the spirituality and the collective vision of the souls who inhabit it. As each soul effects every other soul by its everyday vibrations, the earth is also affected. Just as your soul is in the process of evolving, so is the earth.

"This is why I have told you, Julia, that positive, pure, clear, caring thoughts and acts will keep you in touch with your soul, your direction, and the angelic forces. That will save humanity and the earth from destruction. You and all souls on the earth are at this second directing the earth's future as well as your own."

"Humanity has destroyed itself and the earth many times through its *lack of vision.* You are killed by what you neglect, by what you do not notice and what you do not repair. The earth is destroyed because it is a place without vision. We hope to change this and raise the vibration. The earth was not made to be destroyed."

Hammal paused long enough for me to think about the ultimate lesson of the earth—freedom from boundaries gained through self-love, self-respect, self-compassion and the ability to give respect, love and compassion to all souls.

I thought of how the masters, the angels, were here offering their love, light and vision to our universe. They were trying to teach us how to stay in touch with the truth, our souls, and to travel through the universe on the light while still in physical form.

I understood that the material universe mirrored *all* the souls who inhabited it. Our thoughts—our positive and negative vibrations, our confused or directed knowledge—were all plotting the earth on its course. The earth, too, was a soul evolving to the seventh circle, preparing to enter the first circle of the next level.

The meek shall inherit the earth, shot through my mind.

I reviewed the original plan for the earth. It seemed simple enough—a place to gain knowledge through love and compassion by committing to the core of the earth—learning power through the thinking mind and comprehending love through debt. I knew that the earth was not a place of ultimate spirituality or ultimate power—just a very basic foundation for learning.

Things appeared to go wrong when individuals exercised their free will without knowing where to go, what to do, or by confusing the material world with the reality of the soul. The truth is direction of the soul. It is the spiritual path that ultimately takes us all, sooner or later, back to the Universal Soul and cannot be ignored.

"So *does* it matter if the earth destructs?" I asked.

"Julia, the answer is yes and no.

"It matters or the Cosmic Angelic Force would not be here.

"It matters because it is time for the earth to move on its evolutionary line. If this is not accomplished, the earth will be out of its alignment and will be destroyed.

"It also matters because the individuals that are destroyed *with* the earth will be grieving souls for a long time. This is the real meaning of "the meek shall inherit the earth." Souls will not only grieve, but they will flood the airwaves causing problems in the rest of the universe. Even now, as I have explained, the universe beyond the earth is being affected by the disembodied, grieving souls.

"Every place in the Superstructure has its reason, its direction for being. Each place will continue to repeat itself—the earth will continue to be reborn—until the pattern is no longer needed.

"Ultimately the greater good will resolve the conflict. There is a plan, but the plan changes. No matter how many times the earth is destroyed, it will eventually move on its line and continue on its karmic path. It will eventually balance, go to the next level, and another will take its place.

"The fate of the earth now hinges on the very real forces of Darkness (negative thought and energy) and Light (positive thought and energy). Both exist equally on the planet at this time. To survive, the earth's energy must be rebalanced with clear and directed positive thought and deed.

"Right now, the earth-mind and the minds of all who are on the earth are receiving higher and higher levels of knowledge. Many transmissions in Universal Mind-Thought are initiating currents upon currents, intensely vibrating with increasing speed. This is all according to plan. It is intended to bring the earth to the first circle of the next level, as I have revealed. Unfortunately, this energy has been misunderstood and misinterpreted and a serious war of duelling energies has emerged."

I understood that no matter how many times the earth was destroyed, it would eventually balance and move onto the next level. *Now* is the time to prepare the earth and humanity for the move to the first level of the next circle.

I also understood that nothing in the universe exists without a reason. The earth would continue to be reborn until the "pattern" was no longer needed. For the time being, souls need the earth to work out karma.

So, I thought, the question might better be presented on a more intimate level. The question is should be, "Does it matter if you, personally, become a lost soul that grieves for an eternity?"

If the earth does destruct, approximately six billion souls plus those already clogging the airways will be lost and unable to finish their commitments or be directed. Like the disembodied grieving souls that Hammal interviewed, the souls would not even know they were lost. They would feel only the pain and the chains of their miserable existence.

How long did it take to create the universe in which we now exist—what are the scientific estimates? How long did it take for the matter to come together, for the plants and the trees to grow? How long would it be before the pattern could be repeated, before the ecosystem was again prepared to receive all the souls who were left on the earth at the time of its demise? How long would it be before the souls could pick up where they left off and continue on their path to the light?

Does it matter if the earth destructs? This is a very personal reality, not just an abstract, universal conundrum.

Hammal had nothing more to say.

V
The Plan

"We of the angelic forces cannot continue with the proper placement of the grieving souls. We ask you to help us balance this imbalance."

Samon, Translator to the Physical

Chapter 21
A Gathering of Angels

"Before we can continue achieving a higher goal we must balance through much compassion and understanding." Samon, Translator to the Physical

"Dearest Juleah," Samon, Translator to the Physical was addressing me. I trembled in anticipation. My formal inauguration was beginning. Today I was to learn of "the plan" and *my* function would finally be revealed.

I was acutely aware of the awesome presence of Unga, Farrse, Jake, Mantra and Icail. Hammal powerfully directed the ceremony; always in attendance, it was through him that all the other angels spoke.

"There must be a resource for the growing population of terrorized, lost souls who fly by day and by night, whereby they can pour out their grievances and rid themselves of their grief for the benefit of humankind," Samon continued to speak.

"We of the angelic forces cannot continue with the proper placement of these souls. Juleah, we ask you to help us balance this imbalance."

"Dearest Julia, Samon has addressed you as Juleah because this is your name," Hammal explained. It is how we of the Cosmic Angelic Force know you."

"Whenever a soul is extended cosmically, that extension is named. You, your spirit, your oversoul, is Juleah. Sooner or latter, all souls become named alpha angels.

During my inauguration, I learned that the Cosmic Angelic Force had contacted me simply because I was part of the plan, another cog in the vast machinery of the Cosmic Angelic Force. I was just doing my job, fulfilling my karma, paying the debt that I agreed to undertake prior to coming onto the planet. I questioned no more.

Although I am not at liberty to tell you all of the particulars since the work is universal in nature, I will relay what I can.

As you know, Hammal and the Cosmic Angelic Force are here to bring new information from the cosmos to the earth. The new information will expand the mind of humanity and allow the human race to travel into the cosmos on the spherical forces while still embodied on the earth. The new knowledge will also permit the earth to evolve to the first circle of the next level.

In order to do this the air needs to be cleared of the lost souls. The grieving souls who are in their bodies, and those who have taken over the bodies or ride in the auras of others, have to be addressed.

"We will all be working to help purify the water in the world as well," Hammal said. "This has to do with the souls. If the water goes, then whole nations will go.

"A special seal will be placed on the earth and everything will be sent to its proper place. I will explain this shortly.

"Julia, learn to work with the sun of this planet; it will make your work easier. Start by praying to the sun. Pray for his light to be given to the darkened spirits.

"Pray for the children of the earth. Pray that the light of truth and knowledge can touch the deprived children so that when it is their time they will hold a clear vision of the future and have hope. By this I mean to send out your positive light, direct your energy to all the positive forces that be. It will link your soul with all positive souls and the angelic energy throughout the spherical forces.

"Ask that the cadaverous spirits over the land and sea dissipate.

"Send the animals of the earth the color pink, which is love.

"Continually pray that everything happens as planned so that all are taught in the light of their virtue."

It was mid-February in 1978 when I awakened with the picture of three mountains in my mind. The middle mountain seemed to be of particular interest. It was round and rolling. The one in the rear was high and rugged while that in front seemed more like a plateau. The musical sounding word "Humlich" danced in my brain.

I asked Hammal if this vision and the word "Humlich" held any significance.

"Yes," said Hammal, "The mountains are spiritual places located in the sky, one of which is named Humlich. They were given to the earth by a cosmic princess; their visible reflection is somewhere in Germany."

How curious, I thought. But there was more. When a grieving soul was ready to be cleansed, Hammal disclosed that it was sent to the spiritual mountains.

He revealed that the round, rolling, middle mountain Humlich is a place of purification where one learns reverence and the soul's vitality is rebuilt. The plateau Lubenlich is a place of vision and peace where positive souls gain cosmic understanding about spiritual growth and giving. And the rugged Auhlich is where depressed souls are taught self-worth in order to hold themselves together. "Eventually all grieving souls will touch Humlich before leaving the spiritual mountains," Hammal explained.

"But there is still another place, Pergem," Hammal announced. "It is a mid-ground for grieving souls—a plane in the sky of the visible physical universe. Entities that die suddenly are sent here to spend four days and three nights. Here souls are shown visions of their past lives to gain perspective."

At that moment Samuel, the grieving soul who was not prepared to accept his untimely death, was leaving Pergem, headed for one of the mountains. The angel who accompanied him had mentally taken him through the eight years he had lost so that he could continue on.

During the first weeks of my training, I was asked to wear pinks and purples, the colors of love and spiritual refinement, to help with the incoming vibration.

In preparation for the work, the earth was divided into seven sections, each of which was assigned a particular color and an overseeing angel.

Hammal watches over the United States, Central America and the surrounding waters. Ultramarine blue, a drawing agent, calms and pulls the souls and the countries together.

Unga, Angel of Individual Guidance, oversees South America, part of the South Pacific and all the waters. Fluorescent shimmering orange stimulates pride and serves to awaken past knowledge.

Mantra, Speaker of the Soul, guides the Soviet territories. Pinkeen, a cosmic color, blankets the area to offer comfort and balance within the area; it serves to soften internal tensions and the rigidity of the individuals.

Icail, Bringer of Forseen Knowledge, watches over China, Mongolia, Vietnam, Thailand, Bhutan. Chartreuse surrounds the area to awaken the souls and create balanced harmony.

Burma, Cambodia, Laos, Malasia, Indonesia, Australia, Micronesia, Melanesia, Cambodia, Japan, Korea, the Philippines, New Zealand, part of the South Pacific, NE Land Svalbard (Norway) and Bengladesh are overseen by Samon,

Translator to the Physical. Deep spiritual violet covers these areas.

Sunlight gold settles over Canada, Iceland, Greenland, Arctica and Alaska, offering richness and relaxation. Jake, Speaker of the Lost, protects.

Farrse, Bringer of Universal Colors, watches over Egypt, Iran, Afghanistan, Pakistan, India, Burma, Nepal, Europe, Africa, Turkey, Syria, Iraq, Iran, Saudi Arabia and Israel. The area is surrounded with vio-green, a purple-olive-turquoise, to stimulate rich spiritual harmony and brotherly love.

It was Hammal's job to coordinate all facets of the operation and present the information I needed to send the grieving souls, with their permission, to the proper place to heal. Thereafter they could continue on and my responsibility to them would be over.

Although certain basic colors and angels are assigned to the sections, please do not misunderstand; nothing in the universe is static.

Farrse alone, having great insight and vast knowledge of cosmic color, continually brings new colors and enlightenment to *all* areas of the earth, blessing and offering new knowledge and direction. As Bringer of Universal Color, he can best decide the colors needed for the highest vibration and most delicate balance.

On one occasion Farrse sent yellow to Europe in order to stimulate new thought, and the highest tone of beaded light blue (beaded colors have to do with water and protection) to Israel for spiritual light and protection. He sent India magenta for harmony and forest green to cultivate the mind. Turkey, on this particular day, was sent orange; Syria, red-magenta for thought. Blues, oranges, and pinks were needed to balance the wavelength in Saudi Arabia. Brown-bronze (metals have very high vibrations) went to Iraq. Blue-green was sent to Pakistan; red-brown, for direction and equality, was added to Egypt's color; yellow-orange, for knowledge; turquoise went to Burma for balance and change; pink to Afghanistan. Finland and Sweden received chartreuse for new knowledge and light; Norway was given violet; Iceland red-heat for drive and balance in temperament. England was blessed with veridian green to stimulate harmony and kindness; Scotland received orange. France was offered a pinky-magenta that has blue undertones to help work from the inside out—from thought to manifestation. Portugal needed pink, chartreuse and magenta to stabilize its vibration. Poland required yellow. To help the people of Czechoslovakia work from the earth, Farrse sent burnt umber. Magenta helped to clear thought in Rumania and apricot was sent to Yugoslavia to balance love. Greece received veridian green and Morocco, burnt umber. Italy was wrapped in cerulean blue, a high vibration that is at once peaceful, soothing and active. Hungary was given lavender. East Germany (when it was a separate state) was offered indigo for deep spiritual rest; West Germany received orange and turquoise. Belgium was blessed with subtle, rich, Indian red.

I extend this small vignette, a segment of the activity of one angel to illustrate the ongoing, never-ending work that is forever being offered by the angelic forces. This light, protection and healing is not only afforded to the nations of the earth but to each and every individual at any given moment. The angels are *forever* on guard and ready to help.

I have also been informed that the positions assigned to Hammal's cabinet are not the main functions of the angels, but rather sidelines for this undertaking.

To offer you more insight, working directly under Hammal are angels Camellia, Safronia, Mattir and Haniah. Camellia deciphers and reports the fate of the nations. Safronia congregates the grieving souls of the nations so Mattir is able to determine those who can be helped. Haniah brings the light of wisdom for the lost.

"It is Mattir who gives you your percentages," Hammal informed me, referring to the ratio of grieving souls estimated on any given day.

Unga's firsts in command are Frandairy, Catel, Munsah, Zeriah. Mantra's receives information from Kunan, Flyair, Ununah, Defair.

Icail, Samon, Jake, Farrse and the others likewise have their helpers, who have their helpers, moving out into vast and infinite army.

Angels Mare, Felloy, Leena and Kronfa are channelers, spirits who go around the spherical forces opening up the air spaces.

"Konceeno is one of your guardians, Julia, who is from your birth planet," Hammal announced. "He is the spirit who protects the lost souls that have gone too far over the rims of the earth's atmosphere—the grieving souls that clutter the universe rather than just the earth's airways. Konceeno sends the lost back once they have wandered too far beyond the realm of the angels and their assistants.

"When the negative cones of grieving souls become too full and burst, sending the grieving souls flying into the solar system, it is Konceeno who collects the clusters and prays them back so that they can go to their proper place.

"Julia, you are to say the following to Konceeno once every two weeks: 'Konceeno, with your good judgement, collect and spare the lost souls within your working realm the agony and the pain that is persistent.'

"To the guardians of the mountains say: 'Please help me to direct the souls which Konceeno has looked after so that they may be sent to their proper place.'

"And every morning pray for the grieving souls in general.

"Acaba and Avenu, Unga's black dogs, are also from your birthplace. They travel everywhere with you in this work. They will ward off anything that will ever try to harm you, shielding you and allowing you to delve deeply into the work. They are forever on guard with instant protection. You can't be touched.

"Also remember the name Munada; she will help you. Munada is a great spirit who brings light through the spherical forces, relaying much information to the angels. Munada also helps direct souls with particular problems. When you send your spirit Juleah, Munada goes also. Functioning only with the work of the grieving souls, she brings high energy forces, direction and discipline. She and the selected child or children go together."

Hammal was referring to The Twelve Children Blessings, creative extensions of this solar system that came into being on March 29, 1978. They too, accompany Juleah (my cosmically extended soul) with their grace, helping to clear the air of the grieving souls. They are Erehen, blessing of light; Cameroon, blessing of cleansing rest directed toward peace; Lelnelli, blessing of the heart; Sonita, blessing of freedom; Margarettfz, blessing of peace; Danz, blessing of compassion; Ftzjeb (pronounced Fay-jab), blessing of sight; Carlten Lanaea, blessing of love; Nrebef, blessing of glint; Fontona, blessing of destination; Zooria, blessing of hope; and Lomonia, blessing of the soul, which is an opening of the soul.

"You also have the Cantidas, prayer spirits, whose physicalness is their sound. Eighteen in all, seven are to stay with you at all times. You will be able to send up to eleven every three days to clear the air and prepare the grieving souls to come into the light.

"The Cantidas work on the spirit of the lost souls but affect all souls. They set up a particular vibration within an area or an individual. You must be careful where you send them. Check and double check before you do. If Nrebef, the blessing of glint (which a glimmer of the truth), is sent, Cantidas are usually not needed.

"Ask five Cantidas to accompany Munada at this time. She will direct them to Israel to help the critical situation there.

"Fragrances will help you—the petal of the rose, the petal of jasmine," Hammal continued.

"Colors, gems, beaded things will help. Violet will widen the path and tourmaline will seal the soul to comfort directly. Beaded white light will cleanse and protect."

Hammal paused, then announced, "Julia, you will accompany the head angels of each country no more than two times a week, awake or asleep, to ascertain what is needed. When you accompany the angels, you will see the aura and the physical situation on all levels. You will also be able to see the situation of the grieving souls, including the riders, hangers out, actual and takeovers."

Hammal told me of my function and I was given strict instructions. Meetings were called daily to rehearse a ritual which would become second nature, a ritual that I was told I would be practicing, awake or asleep, for the rest of my life.

Conferences were convened so that I could see how the population of grieving souls fluctuated. Hammal's cabinet reported on the various countries which were under their protection.

I could see that in areas of war, violence and disasters, the numbers of grieving souls increased. And how, after the ritual, the numbers decreased.

The lost souls were summoned and asked if they were ready to forgive themselves and move on. Those that consented went to one of four spiritual places (the three mountains or Pergem) where they could review or rest, release their grievances and renew themselves and their direction. From there, they would continue on to another place of learning, flow into the light to rest in the Universal Soul, or to again return to earth and continue on their karmic path.

Special gifts, protection, light and love were sent into particular areas: flowers, colors, scents, musical notes and spirits to raise the energy of the areas and heal the wounds.

Special prayers were sent for the children, animals and those who were helpless.

The ritual, as much as I have been free to tell you, is followed daily. Percentages relative to the total population in each area are checked. This is broken down as to actual grieving souls, riders, and hangers out. During the ritual, all grieving souls are addressed—the actual grieving souls that grieve in their bodies, those that take up space in the auras or takeover the vehicles of others, and those that hang out in the sky.

The process consists of calling, clearing, praying and blessing.

Special angels on the earth's angelic force clear the baser entities which are sent to their proper place.

I can tell you no more.

Then Hammal said, "We are going to put this seal on the earth and send everything to its proper place." This became my seal of protection. It represents a snake in a fig and looks like this:

The Cosmic Angelic Force is here! The Plan is unfolding. The angels, angelic helpers and spirits of light who have carried love, protection and healing to the earth eternally, continue forever. The force of goodness is not one angel but a gathering of angels—all are here to do the work.

To participate in the flow is unspeakable joy. As part of a perfectly synchronized orchestra, my spirit soars within the full, rich, encompassing harmonies, weaving in and through to infinitely resounding peace...

Epilogue

Prayer and Protection

"We will teach you how to protect your soul, and those you love. We will also teach you how to pray for the earth, the place that gives each and everyone of us our physical presence and livelihood." Hammal Cahone

"Prayer is a gift from the universe. It is a vehicle with which you can align your soul and spirit, enabling you to transcend your physical body.

"With prayer you can enter into a state whereby energy comes to you and flows through you. Through this flow, you become part of the angelic forces. By connecting your energy to angelic energy, you *consciously* work within the light.

"Prayer is a mantra. It is the joining of soul and angelic force to touch a higher soul and direct positive thought to action (energy). In this way, the universe gives you what you want and deserve.

"There are many kinds of prayer, all of which stem from the realization that *there is an answer*.

"Prayer can be *thought*—positive thought—thought with direction.

"Since what you think reflects what you believe, the way in which you act mirrors what you think. This means your *actions* are also prayers.

"Prayer is action, a force, a vibration—true action directed by positive thought. The more positive and directed the action, the clearer and more definite the result.

"Although your thought and actions are prayers, there is far more—prayer is actually the work accomplished through your *total* being. This includes the merest thought to the most carefully rationalized concept. It extends to the simplest way in which you touch anything with your five senses—and even your sixth (which, in its own way, is an extension of prayer). Everything beyond you is prayer and everything within you is a prayer.

"Healing prayer is praying for others with love, good intentions and purity of thought. It allows the light that flows to you, and through you, to heal. It will enhance and strengthen the energy of the one for whom you are praying to the extent that the individual will allow and receive your prayers.

"There is no prayer more powerful than love. To love is to respect and cherish. It is the ultimate prayer. By extending love, you protect and care for that which you love. However, before you can know prayer as love, you must truly know gratitude and appreciation as prayer.

"Appreciation is the recognition that *everything* is a gift, beginning with your life and all that preceded it, to all that you are given on this earth. Life's lessons, joys and pain all allow you to refine your soul and go on to higher levels of truth and light. You must consciously recognize the need to be thankful for everything you are given.

"Total prayer means to walk with the angels—to live continually in a *state of connection* whereby light and goodness will flow to you and through you."

Prayer to Protect the Earth from Decay and Initiate New Growth

Visualize the earth wrapped in *cobalt blue*, then see a layer of *white light* wrapped around the blue.

Pray: May peace and tranquillity radiate out from the center of the earth.

While doing this, picture the following colors radiating from the center of the earth:

Green to neutralize and balance the energy.

Follow with *yellow* to cleanse.

Then see *orange* radiating through the yellow to revitalize.

End with another wash of *green.*

Pray: May peace, enlightenment and vision be brought to the earth. Through this, may all good works be fulfilled.

Say: Thank you. (In saying thank you, you are appreciating yourself, the universe within you, the angelic forces and reinforcing the reverberation of positive thought.)

Prayer to Protect Humanity from Decay

Within your mind visualize your own personal concept of beauty. See *lavender* take its place.

Now picture yourself as the mind of all humanity—extend and *link* your mind to each and every mind on earth.

Send *white light* through your mind and all of your connections. See the white light flow from mind to mind.

Follow this cleansing with *light blue* in the same way.

Pray: Through this light blue, may all positive light pass through humanity. May it collect all negative forces and dissipate them.

Now send the color *canteloupe* (melon) through the minds of all people, giving them a vision of love. As this pinky-peach travels, it will attract any remaining negative energy, pulling it from deep within humankind, causing it to dissolve.

Pray: May this energy cleanse and bring love to all humanity. May it enable a vision of love and all that is good.

Say: Thank you.

Further Reading

For other channeled information from Hammal and the Cosmic Angelic Forces, see <u>Powerful Prayer Secrets: How to Get What You Need Every Day</u>! by Julia Busch and Hollye Davidson, published by Kosmic Kurrents. Learn how the simple psychology of prayer provides the means to overcome guilt, failure, lack of self-worth, and feelings of separation from the universe and a higher power.

<u>Power Color</u>! also by Julia Busch and Hollye Davidson (Kosmic Kurrents) has its basis in color information from Farrse, Bringer of Universal Color. A personality colorscope and individual color-energy primer is contained in this light-hearted approach to deeper meanings.

The H-Files: Conferences with a Cosmic Angel newsletter supplies up-to-the-minute channeled information as it is received from Hammal and the Cosmic Angelic Force. It is available by subscription from Kosmic Kurrents.

Glossary

ageless wisdom truth derived from the Universal Soul.

angel protector; bringer of light.

angel, alpha messenger, guardian with cosmic extensions.

angel, beta messenger, guardian working on earth with no cosmic extensions.

angel, cosmic messenger, protector from beyond the earth.

angel, earth guardian; protector choosing to work and evolve with the earth.

Angelic Force, Cosmic special angelic force sent with a plan to save the earth from destruction.

angelic force(s) light working together; goodness en masse.

animals guardians; pure spirits that cleanse the air with their love.

arc, arch, ark bridge; liaison.

archangel liaison between earth angel and cosmic angel.

auras and planes intense vibrations throughout the solar system; part of the spherical forces.

belief system thoughts reflecting intentions.

Bible book of direction; documented history and future of the earth.

birth incarnation onto the earth.

body vehicle used by the soul to play out its predestined role on earth.

chakra link between physical and cosmic energy.

chronology recordings of linear time; myth.

circle round; completion before moving to the next circle or level.

current force; energy; flow of vibrations.

death continuation of life.

debt god; lord; ruler of the earth; building and balancing; paying and reaping; that which is owed to the universe and the soul; a kink in the soul from the beginning without beginning; karma.

direction reason for being.

duality concept of opposites existing only on earth.

earth place to gain knowledge through love and compassion.

eight see *Meaning of Numbers.*

emotions senses used to weigh personal truths.

etheric double aura closest to the physical body.

Everlasting Perpendicular strongest planal system; the eternal "X" through which angelic light flows.

eyes links with the Universal Soul.

goal of life self-respect; self-love; self-kindness; self-appreciation; end through which love, respect, knowledge, kindness and appreciation is gained for all mankind.

god debt; the earth; rules; universal debt.

good and evil opposites existing only on earth.

genius ability to touch ageless wisdom.

Hammal Cahone Head of the Cosmic Angelic Force assigned to bring new knowledge to the earth.

heaven idea existing only on earth; state in which you are allowed not to pursue; peace; freedom; universal insight gained through karmic work; ultimate point on a karmic path.

heart that which measures the evolution of the soul.

heart, grieving state of indecision.

hell confusion in the mind of humanity.

helpers any and all positive energy.

history directed energy; a forever-existing thought-form.

humor way to release fear; teacher of compassion.

impure yellow careless, confused knowledge.

incarnation soul in a body for the purpose of working out karma.

Infinite which is Infinite Universal Mind-Universal Soul.

intentions, good motions resulting from a positive, expansive belief system.

intentions, ill result of human weakness.

karma result of actions: destiny; cumulative fate; individual work agreed upon in a particular lifetime.

knowledge gift from the Universal Mind.

life on earth direction; focus; role that one plays in order to develop the soul.

light truth; knowledge; goodness.

light and dark opposites existing only on earth.

love kindness; appreciation; respect; vehicle through which knowledge and freedom from boundaries are gained.

mind, individual receptor, conductor of Universal Mind.

Mind, Universal Transmitter of Ageless Wisdom; creative power within; the balance of Universal Soul.

motion any and all vibrations: mental, emotional, physical, universal, cosmic.

negativity attitude resulting from a confused belief system.

nine see *Meaning of Numbers.*

one see *Meaning of Numbers.*

pain teacher; way in which knowledge and truth is learned on the earth, as in "growing pains."

perfection concept resulting from duality.

planal system interdependent levels of energy, e.g., spherical forces; see also auras.

prayer directed positive energy in thought, word and/or deed.

ranoids bubble-like fears in the auras; energy drains equal to seven times the intensity of the original fear squared.

rationalism personal justification via intellectualization.

reality direction of the soul; that which cannot be touched.

seven see *Meaning of Numbers.*

shell physical body; vehicle in which an individual works out karma.

sin limited explanation of hardships humanity imposes on itself;

steps leading to positive growth of the soul.

soul individual direction; truth of understanding; love so clear that one sees because one loves.

soul, directed truth on its path; energy focused by reason for being.

soul, *actual* **grieving** soul that suffers while embodied.

soul, grieving soul unable to touch the angelic forces, universal truth or the light.

soul, *hanger out* **grieving** disembodied grieving soul without a vehicle residing in the airways and blocking the light.

soul, *rider* **grieving** disembodied grieving soul inhabiting an aura.

soul, *takeover* **grieving** disembodied grieving soul residing in a body other than its own.

Soul, Universal purified state of all souls.

spherical forces circular, universal movements united through-out the cosmos by creative energy; auric interpenetrations which include angelic forces and soul energy.

spirit directed energy functioning as an indivisible combina-tion of will, intention, and vision.

spirit, cadaverous residual force of a broken will; dead spirit trapped on earth until the physical body dies.

spirit, vampire destructive, debasing, ravenous force on earth; entity who has been a vampire for many lives.

thought, negative confused belief system rooted in fear and hopelessness; learned bad habit.

thought, positive expansive belief system; thought reflecting good intentions.

time parallel and angular occurrences.

tradition safeguard from reality.

truth kinds and degrees of understanding, such as personal truth, social truth, universal truth.

vampire ravenous entity existing on the earth whose desires cannot be contained.

vibration movement; energy making up currents.

will, free unrestricted ability to act on knowledge.

The Meaning of Numbers

Zero. Nonexistence. Nothingness. The unmanifested. The unlimited. The eternal. The absence of all quality or quantity. The void; non-being. Limitless light. Divine essence. The incomprehensible. The Absolute.

One. The beginning. A reconstruction. The sum of all possibilities. The indivisible. One gives rise to duality, then multiplicity, and back to unity, e.g., one begets two, two begets three, and three begets all things.

Two. Duality. Conflict working toward balance. Polarity, as in good and evil, north and south. Dependence, e.g., man, woman.

Three. Creative power. Expression. Growth. Limitless possibility. Light-sanctifying intelligence. The soul. Duality and unity (one plus two). Has a central point of equilibrium. Multiplicity. One gives rise to two, two gives rise to three, three gives rise to all numbers.

Four. The physical universe. The body. Manifestation. Static as opposed to the circular and dynamic. Completion. Solidarity. Death.

Five. Humanity. Power source—four sides and a point. Door to another level An arc: Arc of the Covenant, Noah's Ark. Source by which new things are pulled or brought onto the planet, e.g., cosmic knowledge. The five books in the Old

Testament—Genesis, Exodus, Levitticus, Deuteronomy and Numbers—had to do with travel to and knowledge from the outer cosmos.

Six. Productivity, physical (four plus two) or spiritual (three plus three).

Seven. Reintegration. Synthesis. Number containing both the spiritual (three) and temporal (four). The completion of a round.

Eight. Spirituality. Paradise regained. Freedom from debt. Nonexistent level in physical manifestation, i.e., nonexistent on the earth. The first circle of the next level.

Nine. Infinity. Truth since it reproduces itself when multiplied. The triple triad. Completion. Fulfillment.

Ten. One plus zero equals one. The beginning, a reconstruction.

Index

seal of protection 180, 188, *188*
seers and auras. *See* auras
self-forgiveness 125. *See also*
    love; respect; appreciation
self-pride 110
self-truth 46
self-worth, place to teach 181
sensations. *See* feelings
seven 21, 127, 109, 162, 163,
    166, 182, 186, 198. *See also*
    circle(s)
sex 47
shell, vacated 147
sickness, alien 28
sin(s) 108–110
    seven deadly 109
six 190, 198
soul(s) 195. *See* also grieving
    souls; vampires
    aligned in cosmic force 69
    as current of exchange 57
    as spherical force 68–69
    beyond the physical 86
    collective vision 174
    confused. *See* thought
    earth-born 145
    eight motions of 109
    energy of as spherical force 68–
    69
    extensions 92–93
    finely attuned 19. *See also* eight
    fragment 96, 145
    functions of 92–97
    group 95–96
    heart and 76
    imbalances in. *See* aura(s);
        spherical force
    kink in 124
    master 92–93, 94
    split 96
    unified 69
    "What is the soul?" 48
Soul, Universal 76, 85, 86, 137

sound
    eternal 23
    power of 23
space, as fluid 66
Speaker of the Lost. *See* Jake
Speaker of the Soul. *See* Mantra
spherical force(s) 25, 63–73 *74*,
    137, 171. *See also* current(s);
        vibration(s); thought
    blockages in 144, 146
    balance of 146
    channeler-spirits 185
    messages via 94
    weakness in 145–146
spirit(s) 100–104. *See also* will
    broken 100–102
    cadaverous 103–104, 181
    changes in 100
    definition 100
    function with soul 100
    great truth and 103
    loss of 101
    nature 149
    strength of 100
    vampire 171

Star Trek 16, 128
sun 180
Superstructure 50

T

TB (tuberculosis) 147, 163
teachers
    children and 127
    of the earth 46–47. *See also* pair
ten 198. *See also* one
thank you 191
thought(s). *See also* mind; Univer-
    sal Mind
    as prayer 189
    blockaded 139. *See also* ranoids
    confused, careless, creative. *See*

Current titles by the author include:

Powerful Prayer Secrets
Positively Young
Power Color
Facelift Naturally
Treat Your Face Like a Salad
Youth and Skin Secrets Revealed

and the bimonthly newsletters:
The H-Files: Conferences with a Cosmic Angel
The *So Young*™: Dedicated to a Youthful Body,
Mind and Spirit

If you wish to write to the author, please write in care of Kosmic Kurrents at the address below; your correspondence will be forwarded. If you wish a response, please include a SASE.

For a complete catalog of titles or for information on jewelry by *Julia*® call 1800 SO YOUNG or write to either:

Julia® *or* Kosmic Kurrents/Anti-Aging Press
P.O. Box 141489
Coral Gables, Florida 33114

TO ORDER

Please send me:

_____ copies MY SECRET LIFE WITH AN ANGEL. $14.95 a copy (plus S&H).

_____ subscriptions THE H-FILES: CONFERENCES WITH A COSMIC ANGEL One
year (6 issues) $15.00 USA. Outside USA $20.50. Up-to-the minute lectures
from Hammal Cahone, Head of the Cosmic Angelic Force.
_____ sample copy $3.50. Outside USA $4.50 (includes S&H).
_____ please include a list of back issues and topics.

_____ copies POWERFUL PRAYER SECRETS. Information from Hammal Cahone.
$9.95 a copy (plus S&H).

_____ copies POWER COLOR. Based on information from the Angel Farrse, Bringer
of Universal Color, relayed through Hammal. $14.95 a copy (plus S&H).

_____ copies of POSITIVELY YOUNG. $9.95 a copy (plus S&H) (book only).
_____ audio programs of POSITIVELY YOUNG. $24.95 a program (plus S&H).

_____ subscriptions *So Young*™: Dedicated to a Youthful Body, Mind and Spirit.
One year (6 issues) $20.00 USA. Outside USA $27.00 (includes S&H).
Holistic health and anti-aging information.
_____ sample copy $4.00 USA. Outside USA $6.00.

____ Free holistic health/anti-aging catalog, includes Facelift Naturally, Treat
Your Face like a Salad, and Special Reports.

____ Free information on jewelry by *Julia*®.

Please include shipping and handling for books and cassettes.
$3.50 for first copy, $2.50 for each additional in USA.
FL residents please add 6.5% sales tax. Enclosed is _____.

Ship to _____

Address_____

City_____

State_____Zip_____

Phone_____

Send your check or money order to
Kosmic Kurrents, P.O. Box 141489, Coral Gables, FL 33114
For more information call
1 800 SO YOUNG